BELLE GUNNESS

BELLE GUNNESS

✝

The Lady Bluebeard

JANET L. LANGLOIS

INDIANA UNIVERSITY PRESS
Bloomington

This book was brought to publication with the assistance of
a grant from the Andrew W. Mellon Foundation.

Manufactured in the United States of America

Library of Congress Cataloging in Publication Data

Langlois, Janet L.
  Belle Gunness.

  Bibliography: p.
  Includes index.
  1. Gunness, Belle, 1859–1908.   2. Crime and
criminals—Norway—Biography.   3. Murder—United States.
I. Title.   II. Title: Belle Gunness.
HV6248.G868L36   1985   364.1′523′0924 [B]   84–43172
ISBN 0–253–31157–8

1 2 3 4 5 89 88 87 86 85

To Lillian de la Torre,
who lent me her notes

CONTENTS

ILLUSTRATIONS

PREFACE AND ACKNOWLEDGMENTS

Writing a book about the folklore surrounding a turn-of-the-century mass murderess is something like trying to catch the ripples caused by a stone once cast into the water. I could not have completed this quixotic adventure without the support of a great many people over the past decade. The journey began with help from faculty and students at Indiana University in Bloomington. Linda Dégh's work on folk legend and community and Richard M. Dorson's work on the place of folklore in American social history have been central to my thinking and led me to formulate an initial fieldwork project in LaPorte, Indiana in 1975–76. Henry Glassie's structural and semiotic analyses of American folk style and Ray DeMaillie's symbolic approach to ethnohistory convinced me that even the simplest story about Belle Gunness, as part of our culture's expressive repertoire, has complex relations to American society.

Grants from the graduate studies and the women's studies programs partially funded my research and so allowed me to explore the connections between a deviant woman's image, folk narrative, and Midwestern cultural ethos. Margaret R. Sheviak and Gary Leonard, both from LaPorte, gave me preliminary information about the community. Files in the Indiana University Folklore Institute Archives, based on student field projects, suggested the extent of community storytelling about the murderess. Interview collections by Claudia David, Ramona Hernandez, Barbara Howes, Julie Hutson, and Janis Mellenthin were particularly helpful.

Perhaps all journeys have a touch of magic or, at least, of the coincidental about them. Fellow student Robie Cogswell found a copy of Lillian de la Torre's 1955 *The Truth about Belle Gunness* in a second-hand store after picking strawberries in southern Indiana at just the time my brother Denis found a copy at an auction in Colorado. Their finds led me to the author, a past president of the Mystery Writers of America, who gave me access to her unpublished 1952 interviews with fifteen LaPorte residents, eyewitnesses to the Gunness events: Isaiah Alderfer, Martha Maxson Alderfer, Eldora Hutson Burns, William Clifford, Frank Coffeen, Frances Lapham Dawson, Emil Greening, N. E. Koch, Evaline Hutson Maxson, Albert Nicholson, Charles F. Pahrman, Dr. Jerold Siegel, Elmore van Winkle, Otto Volheim, and Bessie Folant Worden. Janet Ness, Librarian of the Manuscripts Section, University of Washington Libraries, located relevant letters from the Stewart H. Holbrook collection pertaining to Holbrook's December 1940 trip to LaPorte to gather material for the chap-

ter "Belle of Indiana" in his 1941 *Murder Out Yonder*. Without this comparative material, my own study would be impoverished.

Yet my task would have been impossible without the support of the
LaPorte community. A fortuitous circumstance helped fund my research
there. An interview with Gunness specialist Maxine Ray Ford, a reporter
on the local *LaPorte Herald-Argus*, ended with my landing a job on the
paper. I was able to use the clipping library, most appropriately in this
case called a "morgue," and to talk with editors Don Benn and Forbes
Julian about the political history of the community. Ruth Tallant, curator,
and Evelyn Nordyke, staff member, of the LaPorte County Historical Society Museum were tireless in supplying me with legal documents pertaining to the Gunness case and in suggesting persons to interview. The
museum pamphlet *The Gunness Story* was instrumental in summarizing
the community story. LaPorte historians Martin Barlag, Robert and Ruth
Andrew Coffeen, Eugene McDonald, and Dorothy Rowley shared their ex-
pertise, while eyewitnesses Louis H. Blake, Eldora Hutson Burns, Mabel
Carpenter (pseud.), Carrie Garwood Davis, Lucia Racher Egle, Almetta
Hay, George Heusi, Henry Johnson, Frank Kerwin, Glenn Ott, Dora
Diesslin Rosenow, and Mary Swenson (pseud.) told me their experiences
one more time. Barb Collins, Art Flickinger, Alfred Fox (pseud.), Orvil R.
Hartle, Linda Hoffer, Fred Hoffman, Jake and Susie Jones (pseud.), Jane
Shoemaker, Suzanna Smith (pseud.), and Martin Swanson shared stories
that they had learned from family and friends about the mass murderess
and her effect on their town. Glenn Linneman, an English instructor at
LaPorte High School, administered a questionnaire to his classes which
gauged younger residents' knowledge about Belle Gunness. Two of his students, Steven James and Jeff Zirzow, consented to fuller interviews.

Harold Poe, recently retired from the Department of Theater and Speech
at the University of Southwestern Louisiana at Lafayette, and originally
from LaPorte, allowed me to quote from the script of his play *Gnista*.
LaPorte High School students Megan Backus and Jerry Snyder discussed
their participation in one of the productions of the play. Juanita Schnable,
known for playing the role of the murderess in several town skits, also
discussed her part in creating the Gunness image on stage.

Robert F. Cutler, Jr. allowed me to read the Cutler Funeral Home records 1902–1908 for information concerning funeral arrangements for
Gunness family members and other Gunness victims. John Nepsha, Jr.
gave me permission to read the abstract of the property once belonging to
the murderess and the place where all her victims were found. I thank all
the people mentioned here and all the other residents of LaPorte for making my stay in their community so pleasurable.

Other people helped me, too. Norwegian historian Kjell Haarstad at the

University of Trondheim sent information on Gunness's early life in Selbu, Norway and her emigration to the United States, while Dorothy Budsberg Honeck and Donald Woodford, descendants of two of Gunness's victims, made their family stories about the murderess available. Jerrold Gustafson, Assistant Audio-Visual Librarian at the Michigan City (Indiana) Public Library, arranged for me to listen to the oral history cassette collection of LaPorte County, prepared under a CETA grant in 1977–79.

A Wayne State University Faculty Research Award in 1981 allowed follow-up research at the LaPorte County Museum, the Newberry Library, and the Chicago Public Library for revisions of my doctoral dissertation, which was completed in 1977. The revisions incorporate readings in American community history and women's studies, as well as in symbolic anthropology and semiotics. Barbara Babcock's work on symbolic inversion, the way in which a culture can reverse its norms and values through symbols, informs the general pattern of this book, while Natalie Zemon Davis's discussion about the figurative use of the disordered woman in preindustrial Europe is both the particular point and the counterpoint to the argument presented here. The hypothesis that stories about Belle Gunness signify complex community attitudes towards urbanization and modernization, however, is my own, for which I take sole responsibility.

At journey's end, the traveler's reward is most often embodied in a loving spouse with whom one lives happily ever after. I give final thanks to my husband, Andrea di Tommaso, who encouraged me to finish this project at last.

BELLE
GUNNESS

INTRODUCTION

BRICOLAGE

The greatest number of murders ever ascribed to a modern murderess is 16, together with a further 12 possible victims, making a total of 28. This was the case of
Bella Paulsdatter Sorensen Gunness (1859–1908) of LaPorte, Indiana. Evidence
came to light when her farm was set on fire on April 28, 1908, when she herself was
found by a jury to have committed suicide by strychnine poisoning. Her victims,
remains of many of whom were dug from her pigpen (her maiden name was Grunt),
are believed to comprise two husbands, at least eight and possibly 20 would be
suitors lured by "Lonely Hearts" advertisements, three women and three children.

Guinness Book of World Records[1]

NOTHING SEEMS MORE SUCCINCT than this entry listed under the
category "Most Polific Murderers" in twelve editions of the *Guinness Book*. Yet a closer look at the text shows gaps. Belle Gunness's
victims are only believed to number twenty-eight. Many of her
suitors remain merely possibilities. These textual ambiguities reflect the historical uncertainties surrounding the immigrant
Norwegian farm woman who put an American town on the map at
the turn of the century.

Little is known of her life, either before or after she moved to the
northwestern Indiana farm in the fall of 1901 that would be called
"Murder Hill" for decades after. A patchwork piecing-together of
her pre-1901 biography reveals the rents in the documented information about "the Lady Bluebeard" of the Middle West.[2] Norwe-

gian historian Kjell Haarstad writes that she was born Brynhild
Paulsdatter Størset (and not "Grunt," as the *Guinness Book* entry
states) on November 11, 1859 in the fishing and farming hamlet of
Innbygde in the town of Selbu on the west coast of Norway, not far
from the city of Trondheim. Her father, Paul Pedersen, a *husmann*
or cotter, was one of the poorer sharecroppers in the community.
He leased a small farm, "Størsetgjerdet," at the bottom of the val-
ley leading to the lake of Selbu. There he raised a few cows, sheep,
and goats, as well as a meager supply of barley, oats, and potatoes
which scarcely fed his wife and children. Although Pedersen
worked as a stone mason to supplement the family income, especially during the winter months when his farm duties lightened, he
was deemed below the poverty level by the town authorities and
received poor relief at least once, in April 1878, when his youngest
daughter, Brynhild, was eighteen.

Once news of the Indiana murders reached Selbu, town residents
recalled Brynhild's early life in quite different ways. Some, such as
the religious instructor who had confirmed her in the Evangelical
Lutheran Church in 1874 and the farmer for whom she had worked
until 1881, remembered that her behavior had been exemplary.
Others' attitudes were expressed in an editorial comment which
appeared in the local newspaper *Selbyggen* in 1908: "Here in Selbu
she is remembered by many, and mostly they tell that she was a
very bad human being, capricious and extemely malicious. She had
unpretty habits, always in the mood for dirty tricks, talked little
and was a liar already as a child. People mocked her and called her
'Snurkvistpåla.'"

Although Haarstad finds it difficult to evaluate the divergent
traditions of the "good Brynhild" and the "bad Brynhild" (traditions that persist in the American context), he sees the community
label "Snurkvistpåla" as quite probable. The nickname, which
fused *snurkvist* (spruce twigs) with *påla* (Paul's daughter), was
both descriptive and pejorative. As a young girl, Brynhild had apparently collected kindling for her family, most often the twigs
from the fast-burning spruce which grew up the mountain slopes.
This task signaled the family's poverty, for it showed that they
could not afford the more usual hardwoods for their fires. One can
conjecture, then, that indigence and humiliation made her childhood a difficult one, even though there is no record of the effect this
naming had on Brynhild herself.

Around the time that she was fourteen, in 1874, she was hired out to surrounding farms as a cattle girl or dairy maid. Like other unmarried girls, she must have taken her employers' cattle to forage above the hamlet in mountain pastures for the summer months. Life in the *seters*, or mountain farms, meant early rising to milk the cows, herding of cattle through the day, and evenings spent bedding down the animals. It meant churning the cream into butter and making cheese to fill the farmers' larders. Her last employer, the farmer Rødde, remembered that she had been a hard worker.[3]

Storytelling must have relieved the monotony. Perhaps she talked with the other girls about the legendary *huldre* women, those fairy creatures whose cows' tails revealed their inhuman natures to their mortal husbands, or about the *gjöyer*, the female trolls who lumbered through the mountains. They may have spoken too about the husbands who had the power to shapeshift into monstrous bears. Perhaps they didn't speak at all, but the teenage dairy maid grew into a woman whose malevolence seemed to match that of the unseen beings peopling Norwegian folk tradition.[4]

Skilled storytellers may have passed through the *seters*, filling the summer nights with *eventyr*, magical tales about heroes and heroines who surmounted impossible odds to win wealth and aristocratic marriages at last. Perhaps because the style of telling tales in Norway's western counties was short and to the point, the fictional tales had the patina of reality. For many listeners, the other world of the folk tales must have merged with that new world across the sea. In Norwegian novelist Ole Rölvaag's *Giants in the Earth*, Per Hansa sees his move to the Dakota plains as the living out of a fairytale; he calls himself *Askelad*, or "Ash Boy," the hero of many Norwegian folk tales. H. A. Foss's *Husmandsgutten (The Cotter's Son)* was a popular romance among Norwegians on both sides of the Atlantic at the end of the nineteenth century, precisely because it translated the fairytale quest into a success story. A poor cotter's son, rejected as a rich girl's suitor, makes money in America and returns to Norway to marry her and save her ruined estate. Railroad companies' brochures and Norwegian emigrants' letters home confirmed the connection by speaking of America as the land of opportunity where the rags-to-riches myth came true.[5]

Brynhild must have shared hopes of a golden future with the

thousands of young, unmarried Norwegians of both sexes who flocked to American cities at the turn of the century, for she emigrated on the steamship *Tasso* sometime after 1881. Her destination was listed as Chicago, her occupation as servant girl on the emigrant protocol papers. Her older sister Olina (Nellie) Larson, who had emigrated earlier and married in the city, paid for her passage. Brynhild probably arrived sometime in 1883. Perhaps she changed her name to "Bella" or "Belle" soon after her arrival. All extant documents carry the latter signature, so she must have anglicized her name, as her sister had before her, in an attempt to "be American."[6]

Because servant girls could dress like the ladies they served, the class differences in the industrialized Middle West may not have been immediately apparent to her. Despite the fact that she, like other immigrant women, faced the worst discrimination in terms of unskilled jobs available, long hours, low pay, and unhealthy working conditions, she may have felt that sewing piecework and doing laundry were the obligatory tasks one moved through in realizing the American dream.[7]

It is hard to say when the dream began to shatter for her. True to the pattern of fairytale and of social mobility, she appeared to marry up when she wed Norwegian Mads Sorensen in 1884, when she was twenty-five. Her wedding picture shows a respectable young woman dressed in black, perhaps taffeta or silk moire, with lace ruffles and a triple strand of pearls around her neck. As her left hand is crossed over her right, her double wedding bands are emphasized and become the central focus of the portrait.

Yet mystery writer Lillian de la Torre, in her 1955 *The Truth about Belle Gunness*, and social historian Ann Jones, in the chapter on Belle in her 1980 *Women Who Kill*, found contradictory accounts of her first marriage. Some reports suggest that the couple were poverty-stricken and ill fated, others that they had a great deal of money. Mads, a watchman or department store guard when they first married in Chicago, must have had a steady working-class income, but one that paled in comparison to that of industrial magnates such as Marshall Field, Potter Palmer, and George Pullman, who embodied the Victorian success ethic. After twelve years of moving from one inexpensive apartment to another, the couple moved to a blue-collar fringe of the wealthy Chicago suburb of Austin in 1896. There, Mads worked for the Chicago and North-western Railroad for only twelve to fifteen dollars a week.

Yet a *LaPorte Argus-Bulletin* editorial of May 7, 1908 noted that Mads "provided with lavish hand for every want of his wife, dressing her handsomely, providing her with jewels, and in every way satisfying the little ambitions so inseparably linked with womanhood." Nellie Larson, possibly estranged from her sister for some years, was quoted as saying, "My sister was crazy for money. That was her great weakness. As a young woman she never seemed to care for a man for his own self, only for the money or luxury he was able to give her. When living with her first husband in Austin, she used to say, 'I would never remain with this man if it was not for the nice home he has'" (*Chicago Tribune*, 7 May 1908). She told reporters that her sister had "lots of money and property and loved life" but that she did "not know where she got all of her money" (*LaPorte Argus-Bulletin*, 7 May 1908).

Some answers to this seeming paradox set up a depressing, interlocked pattern of probable arson for fire insurance premiums and murder for life insurance benefits that Belle would appear to duplicate later in Indiana. Jones, using the *Chicago Tribune*'s coverage as her main source, found that the confectioners' shop Belle opened in 1896 on the corner of Elizabeth and Grand avenues in Chicago burned down less than a year after its opening. Belle told the insurance investigators that a kerosene lamp had exploded and set the place on fire. Despite the fact that the lamp was not found in the wreckage, the premiums were paid. It was this money, Jones conjectures, which allowed the Sorensens to buy their first house in Austin. This house, too, burned down, in 1898, and they collected once again. De la Torre writes that a third house burned down as well before Mads and Belle settled in their last house, at 621 Alma Street.

Jones notes that two of Belle's four children died in the very years the fires occurred. Her oldest child, Caroline, died in 1896, and her first son, Axel, in 1898. Both children were infants; both had symptoms of acute colitis—or of poisoning—and both were insured.

And it was in the Alma Street house, after seventeen years of marriage, that Mads died one summer day in 1900—July 30, the one and only day that two life insurance policies with two different mutual benefit associations overlapped. Dr. J. B. Miller of Chicago recalled for reporters in 1908 that he had been a young medical student who had once boarded with the Sorensens. He was called to the Austin home that day and found Mads dying with the characteristic symptoms of strychnine poisoning. Belle told him that she had given Mads a powder to help his cold. The Sorensens' family physician, C. E. Jones, assured Miller that he had been treating Mads for an enlarged heart, so that no autopsy was needed. And so Miller signed the death certificate showing that Mads had died of natural causes. The insuring fraternal associations did not ask for an autopsy either; they awarded Belle $8,500, with which she purchased the farm on the outskirts of LaPorte.

The LaPorte editorial of May 7, 1908 attributed Belle's later murders overtly to her marriage in Chicago and covertly to her immigration experience. It contrasted the purity of her childhood in Norway with the bestiality of her life in America:

> There was nothing in her nature as a girl which in any way forecast the career of crime she was fated to live in the later years of her life. She was a woman of apparently an intense religious nature, with a passion for doing good. This was a predominant element in her character up to the time she became affianced of Max Sorenson [Sorensen]. It was while living with him that she developed the element of her nature which had been slumbering for the commission of crime, for the apparent gratification of her desire to accumulate wealth.

Nellie Larson confirmed the connection between Belle's first marriage and the murders of her later suitors in a mystical way when she told reporters that she had last seen her sister at Mads's funeral over seven years before. "While I was there a terrible feeling came over me. I felt just like something terrible was going to happen and I could not stand up. Now I see what it meant. There has been found a lot of dead people on my sister's land. I don't understand it" (*LaPorte Argus-Bulletin*, 7 May 1908).

Perhaps Belle was "an industrious Norwegian immigrant imbued with the thoroughly American drive to make money," as Ann Jones sees her (p. 129). Perhaps, when she found that her first marriage did not meet her expectations, she so twisted the dream through the "marriage-and-murder" racket she apparently perfected in Indiana that she created her own monstrous version of fairytale success.

When Belle came to LaPorte, her life intersected with the town's. The woman and the community each had a separate identity until that fateful autumn when their histories merged.[8] Some of LaPorte's 10,000 residents knew the superficial outline of their new neighbor's life. They knew that she had been born in Norway and that she had come to town as the Widow Sorensen with a foster daughter, Jennie Olsen, and her two surviving children, Myrtle (born in 1897) and Lucy (born in 1899). As time passed, they knew that she married a Norwegian farmer, Peter Gunness, the April after she had settled on the farm, and that he was dead less than a year later, in December 1902. They knew, too, that she gave birth to a son, Philip, the following spring and that her foster daughter, Jennie, left for a finishing school in California in 1906. And they knew that the Widow Gunness worked the farm with the help of a succession of hired hands after her husband's death and that she had a number of out-of-town visitors during those years as well.

When Belle's farmhouse burned down in the early morning of April 28, 1908, people realized how little they knew about the Mistress of Murder Hill. Many assumed that the four bodies found in the farmhouse's smoldering basement were Belle's (with head missing) and her three children's (Myrtle, Lucy, and Philip). Many felt that the LaPorte County sheriff was correct in arresting Ray Lamphere, a handyman Belle had hired in 1906 and fired the previous February, as the prime suspect on charges of murder and arson. When more bodies, dismembered, covered with lye, and wrapped in gunny sacks, were discovered on the farmgrounds a week later, they weren't so sure what to think.

It dawned on most, with horror, that their neighbor had been a mass murderess. The bodies of Andrew Helgelien, a rancher from Aberdeen, South Dakota who had come to visit Belle in January, and of Jennie Olsen were the first unearthed. Yet they were quickly followed by others. The bodies of an unidentified woman and at least four more men (accounts vary) were also uncovered in the mass of human bones, bone fragments, and personal items, such as men's watches, which turned up in the digging. Hired men Eric Gurhold and Olaf Lindblom were identified. So were the bodies of John Moo (or Moe), a farmer from Elbow Lake, Minnesota, and Ole Budsberg, a farmer from Iola, Wisconsin. The men, representative of the Norwegian communities spread across the

United States, had answered Belle's matrimonial advertisements referred to in the *Guinness Book* entry. None had ever left the farm, except George Anderson from Tarkio, Missouri, who counted himself extremely lucky afterwards to have kept his savings and his life.

Glenn Ott, who skipped three weeks of school when he was thirteen to watch the excavations of bodies at the Gunness place, said that he didn't "know how to place it," that complex community event of murder.[9] Nor did anyone else. For people have talked about the murders around family dinner tables, on front porches, during coffeebreaks, at barber shops and club meetings, and on the benches set on the courthouse lawn in the center of town for over seventy-five years. They have talked to each other and to interested outsiders, newspaper reporters, detective story writers, and university researchers (myself included) for decades in attempts to understand what happened.

In the face of Belle Gunness's inexplicable presence in their community, they have had to literally build her history (and with it their own) from fragmented and contradictory evidence. They have had to become what anthropologist Claude Lévi-Strauss calls *bricoleurs*, handymen themselves piecing together the unknown world of a disordered woman in their midst. Talking together seems to have helped townspeople over the years to sort out elements of a baffling situation that would otherwise remain unintelligible to them. Faced with chaos, what anthropologist Clifford Geertz has defined as "a tumult of events which lack not just interpretations but interpretability," they have had to construct verbal images of their community's encounter with mass murder.[10]

This joint fabrication of the past, seen as necessary to a group's self-definition and cohesion by symbolic anthropologists and sociologists of knowledge, partially explains journalist Stewart H. Holbrook's observation: "Of all the many Bluebeards of both sexes the United States has produced, none I believe has been the subject of more comment, or the source of more folklore than Mrs. Gunness." Intrigued by the ballads he found circulating about the murderess when he visited LaPorte in a 1940 field trip for his book *Murder Out Yonder: An Informal Study of Certain Classic Crimes in Back-Country America*, Holbrook predicted accurately that "Belle Gunness, in fact, seems assured of an enduring place in the folklore of the region."[11] Personal reminiscences, family stories, community legends, jokes, anecdotes, ballads, and plays—in a word, verbal folk art—have become finely honed tools in building up histories useful in staving off the incomprehensible. Here, the distinction between history as documented fact and folklore as false or exaggerated information blurs in the culturally framed attempt to construct reality.

In his 1971 article "Defining the American Folk Legend," Richard M. Dorson has written that "murder is one of the complex events in community life most apt to generate local traditions," precisely because it is one of those extraordinary phenomena around which community folk art is shaped as a strategy for comprehension. Linda Dégh and Andrew Vázsonyi have found that most legend-telling situations can be reduced to people's "making inferences that strive to reach conclusions from premises" about reality in the face of the very events which shake the categories of the real generally shared. And so this book becomes more a record of people coping with the Belle Gunness phenomenon through the symbolic medium of folk art than a record of the murderess herself.[12]

Yet Dégh and Vázsonyi have also found that propositions about reality, even in a given community, are rarely uniform and usually debatable, so that folk art develops in a dialectic.[13] Certainly, the structuring process in LaPorte has been a dialectical one. With the exception of the date of the farmhouse fire, almost every sentence in the *Guinness Book*'s account has been contested. LaPorte residents have disagreed about the number of Mrs. Gunness's victims, who they were, and how she killed them. They have argued about the person who really set that April 1908 fire, although Ray Lamphere was found guilty of arson at a November 1908 trial and sentenced to the Northern Indiana State Penitentiary, where he died of tuberculosis a year later. They have discussed, pro and con, the possibility that Belle might have escaped her burning house to enjoy the wealth obtained from her unfortunate suitors, even though the LaPorte County coroner pronounced hers to be the decapitated body found in the farmhouse ruins. Furthermore, there is evidence that debates have reverberated throughout the town from the moment news of the murders first surfaced. Glenn Ott told me that "everybody had different ideas on it, you know." And Martin

Barlag, whose stepmother had waited on Belle in one of the town's grocery markets, finished a story and said, "Now, see, that influenced me because I heard it from my Mom. Someone else heard a different version from someone else, why, they'd have a little different slant on it."[14]

When Lillian de la Torre wrote *The Truth about Belle Gunness* for the Fawcett Gold Medal series on famous criminal trials in 1955, she based her interpretation on an analysis of relevant legal documents, eyewitness accounts, and previous publications. Although *The Truth* plausibly resolves much of the historical mystery surrounding the murderess by synthesizing opposing views on the nature of the case, the arguments continue. Belle Gunness has remained an intriguing topic for conversation into the 1980s. One possible reason why the Gunness phenomenon has such a contradictory, yet enduring, place in the community memory is related to the social nature of folk art, which leaves spaces open for what Alfred Schutz has called "multiple provinces of meaning." In order to understand their past, people of different ages, sexes, occupations, and political persuasions, at different points in time, have created variable images of the deviant woman and the events which threw their town into the limelight. In so doing, they have invested the murderess's image and the historical events themselves with many meanings dependent on these social and cultural differences.[15]

Symbolic anthropologists Janet Dolgin and JoAnn Magdoff have noted that communities often turn their respective histories into "invisible events" that become submerged within current concerns. "As time passes," they write, "events of import to a people, redolent with detail, retain only the skeleton of their significance or, having lost much of their previous content, these events become vehicles for new significations." They continue, "At the same time, such events embody contemporary meanings, legitimated by an implicit reference to a historic past; simultaneously, they (event-meaning) legitimate the past by exemplifying its continuity in the present."[16] Something of this dual process of legitimization appears to have occurred in LaPorte. Townspeople have turned the Gunness Horror into a complex metaphor, into a multivalent presence that ultimately defines their community itself, through their emptying and filling the historic events with a succession of significances over time.

Victor Turner has shown that historic events can be read by both participants and analysts as social dramas which reveal broad cultural conflicts in the condensed and usable forms of metaphor. Stories about these events bring the drama to a second level of symbol in narrative form. Robert Georges, in fact, has defined folk legends, and by extension the verbal art of all folk performances, as "metaphorizations of basic kinds of relationship sets . . . incapable of being tested empirically to the satisfaction of every man." A case can be made for approaching the debate-laden stories about Belle Gunness as "ethnographic miniatures" of problematic "wall-sized culturescapes," to borrow Clifford Geertz's artistic imagery.[17]

A preliminary point in favor of this approach comes from Lillian de la Torre's analysis of her own interest in criminal behavior. After she had completed research on the Gunness case, she wrote that "the intense light generated when human relationships burst into flame in some great crime leads to the illumination of man's soul, man's proper study." Her statement, which suggests the power of deviant acts to explain human culture in all its complexity, complements historian Louise Tilly's plea that social scientists studying women consider the negative or anomalous cases in order to understand the boundaries of appropriate cultural roles for all. In the introduction to her *Victorian Murderesses: A True History of Thirteen Respectable French and English Women Accused of Unspeakable Crimes*, Mary S. Hartman notes that "Durkheim's brilliant formula that the deviant person is created by and necessary to the community, both as a focus for group feelings and as an indicator of prevailing social boundaries and behavior, is now a commonplace." She goes on to say: "Taking a human life, of course, has always been considered an extreme form of deviancy in most societies, but even with the accused murderer, as with all lesser deviants, community attitudes and modes of control vary immensely and depend upon many factors" (p. 10). From this perspective, a woman murdering, then, becomes a negative metaphor depicting a wide variety of community value systems and control mechanisms.[18]

Like the topos of the disordered woman that historian Natalie Zemon Davis found prevalent in the folk art of preindustrial Europe, the image of Belle Gunness emerging in LaPorte's folk traditions symbolically inverts many of the cultural norms that have made up the fabric of traditional communities, epitomized in American life by the small town. And the small town is one of the dominant images in our culture. Park Dixon Goist, whose book *From Main Street to State Street: Town, City, and Community in America* analyzes "this powerful cultural myth of the town," sees that the myth "still remains a pervasive force in the way we see things," regardless of the changing realities of American urbanization, a process already underway in the 1850s.[19]

Unlike the situation that Natalie Davis analyzed, however, the complexity of the industrial and postindustrial Midwest precludes an image of deviance shared by all and fosters a figure created in conflict and debate. The dialectic over the image of Belle Gunness in LaPorte imperceptibly merges with what Goist has called "one of the truly important cultural dialogues in America," the debate over the definition of community in a culture caught between the myth of the small town and the image of the city (p. 164). The following chapters are arranged so that community folk art highlights the tension between the woman who broke all the rules that ideally organized social life and the small town that tried to keep them in the face of broad social and economic changes.

Part 1 presents the town's sense of disintegration. These first two chapters explore Belle Gunness's subversion of the codes of neighborliness and hospitality, which ultimately corroded community values while foreshadowing the shift to urban sensibilities. Part 2 explores the mass murderess's annihilation of community patterns of sexual roles, marriage, and kinship. This destruction of social mores, strikingly parallel to urban shifts in these areas, is encoded in stories about her sexual ambiguity, her marital relationships, and the procedures she used in killing her victims. Chapter 4, "The Lady Bluebeard," is a pivotal one, because it traces the historical shift in the metaphors used to describe her murders, which is ultimately a shift in the metaphors used to describe sexual meaning in a Midwestern context.

The two chapters in part 3 outline the breakdown of community economic and political codes. The process begins with Belle Gunness's marriage racket, which applied big-city business tactics to the domestic sphere hallowed in small-town family life. It ends with the possible collusion of law officers in her criminal activities. The last chapter, "Belle Gunness Is Alive and Well," places the major dialectic about Belle's death in, or escape from, her farm-house fire in the framework of the two-party political system which has defined the community sense of American democracy since the institution of Fourth of July parades and picnics.

The idea that folk images of the mass murderess chart a community's contradictory response to modernization, industrialization, and urbanization is an act of *bricolage* itself. The researcher, like the townspeople sorting out the evidence of Belle Gunness's crimes, analyzes data which are, as Clifford Geertz has noted, "superimposed upon or knotted into one another . . . at once strange, irregular and implicit." The analysis is a second-order interpretation at best. Yet, when people study people, the complexities of cultural structures have to be unraveled, even in the simplest way, for fuller understanding. In order to keep the interpretation of symbolic forms rooted in concrete folk artistry, individual voices have been left to present their own stories of the woman turned upside down.[20]

PART I

†

Community Disorder

† 1 †

"BELLE GUNNESS PUT US ON THE MAP"

THE LITERAL MAP

LaPorte, now a third-class city of 22,000 people in northwest Indiana, has officially been on the map since 1832, when it was named the seat of the newly incorporated LaPorte County because of the boosterism of its founding fathers. The five men—Walter Wilson, Hiram Todd, John Walker, James Andrew, and Abram P. Andrew, Jr.—had bought 400 acres of Indiana land at a land sale in late 1831 in exchange for scrip given the Andrew brothers for their engineering work on the Michigan Road. Although its early residents were of English and Scots-Irish descent from the eastern seaboard states (primarily New England and New York) or from other states in the Northwest Territory, the name the French trappers had taken from the Potawatomi for the nearby entrance to the Sauk Trail remained: "LaPorte" ("the Door").

From the 1850s through the 1870s, the original settlers were joined by German and Irish immigrants as a result of the transcontinental development of the railroad, which reached LaPorte County in 1852. After the Civil War, Southern black workers joined the immigrants in the railway machine shops and the Fox Woolen Mills, which kept the town's economy afloat in the recession following the boom time of the war. Economic disaster struck, however, when the Michigan Southern Railroad Company pulled its shops out of LaPorte and relocated them in Elkhart, Indiana, in 1870. The town's population declined slightly in the following years, although diversified industry, such as the ice-harvesting trade, and professional and service businesses flourished.

Just before World War I, Polish immigrants and Southern blacks came to LaPorte to work for the Advance-Rumely Company, founded by German immigrants Meinrad and John Rumely in 1853 to capitalize on the railroad boom. The company was expanding its production of the farm machinery purchased by county farmers to meet the expanded need for crops and livestock during war time. After the war, the economy dipped to the Depression of the 1930s. The county and the county seat were hard hit. Farms were foreclosed; the Advance-Rumely Company went into receivership because of unpaid bills; former factory workers stood in bread lines. The town of LaPorte qualified for WPA assistance in those years.

During World War II, the economic picture brightened considerably. The Allis-Chalmers Manufacturing Company, which had taken over the ailing Advance-Rumely Company, replaced production of farm equipment with manufacture of antiaircraft guns for the war's duration. Both Southern blacks and Southern whites came north to do war work there and at the now-defunct Kingsbury Ordnance Plant south of town. County farmers increased livestock production to the point that more hogs were raised and shipped to markets in the 1940s than at any other time.

The town has been a summer resort since the nineteenth century. Conductors once stopped the trains to point out the town's lakes—North and South Pine, Clear, Stone, and Fish Trap—to their passengers. Chicago families still have summer cottages on the Pine, and the Holiday Inn there is a regional center for business meetings and conferences. Yet LaPorte's industrial park, made up of over fifty-five manufacturing and processing plants, and Allis-Chalmers, the largest employer in LaPorte until its close in 1983, have not been able to compete with the massive steel industry built up in Burns Harbor, Gary, and Hammond, Indiana in the postwar period. These major urban industries have drained LaPorte's population, which has remained relatively stable since the 1940s. Most of its residents are white (90 percent), and many have been born and raised in the region, despite the influx of immigrants and migrants in its 150-year history.[1]

THE SYMBOLIC MAP

The city of LaPorte is presently divided into five administrative wards. Just as W. L. Warner found for Yankee City (Newburyport, Connecticut) and Robert and Helen Lynd found for Middletown (Muncie, Indiana), its districts can be seen as spatial symbols of the community's historical development.[2] They outline its social, political, religious, and economic divisions to a surprising degree. The prestigious Third Ward, for example, is in the center of town on the site of the original settlement. It contains *the* avenues, Indiana and Michigan, whose beautiful old homes shaded by magnificent maples reflect the high social status of their owners. Residents in this ward tend to be members of the oldest families in LaPorte, to vote Republican, to belong to churches of Protestant denominations, and to be the Anglo-Saxon professional and business elite.

In contrast, residents in the First Ward, which is still called "Pole Town" and once was home to Irish, German, and early black townspeople, and in the Fifth Ward, which has a large Southern population dating from the 1940s, tend to vote Democratic. Many belong to the Roman Catholic church and are in the lower-income brackets. These wards contain working-class neighborhoods which are old and well established.

Residents in the Second and Fourth wards tend to be a mixed group on all levels and represent the newest areas of expansion into a limited suburbia. Their demographic patterns indicate that ward boundaries are not absolutely rigid and are becoming blurred as time goes on.[3]

The town is the hub of a wheel of surrounding rural townships and farmlands in the county. Its central geographic location symbolizes its economic dominance over, yet dependence on, the small farming communities of Fish Lake, Hanna, Hudson Lake, New Carlisle, Rolling Prairie, Union Mills, and Wanatah. LaPorte is embedded in a crisscrossing network of country roads, which divide and connect farms producing corn and sorghum crops, grapes, and wine in the sandy soil south of Lake Michigan. County farms, many of them in the same family for over one hundred years, are known for their dairy and pork products, as well. Allis-Chalmers's production of farm implements and the American Home Produce Company's processing of farm produce have been only two examples of the complex interconnection of town and country.

At the same time, LaPorte is enclosed within a triangle formed by much larger urban industrial centers. South Bend is twenty-six miles to the east, Michigan City twelve miles to the north, and the Gary-Hammond-East Chicago-Chicago megalopolis forty-five miles to the west. This geographic position, too, has symbolic implications. Like other small cities in a mass society, LaPorte has been wedged out of certain economic markets yet depends on large cities for commerce. Allis-Chalmers farm implements, Lay Trucking Company products, Whirlpool Corporation service parts, Scotts-Foresman educational publications, and Boise Cascade cardboard packaging, for instance, have a national and international market, yet LaPorte is valued for its "country charm" by the urbanites who summer there.

Its somewhat paradoxical position in at least two superimposed landscapes—one rural and one urban—is turned to a positive value in a recent Chamber of Commerce publication, quoted rather extensively below:

> The following pages will give a description of an unusual community—a vital and thriving industrial city, but one still retaining much of the charm and easy living so characteristic of the Middle West of several decades ago.
>
> Located in the center of LaPorte County, and serving as the seat of county government, LaPorte lies within an area of ever-expanding commerce and trade. And yet, on a summer's afternoon, a stroll under LaPorte's famous maple trees, or the sharp "pop" of a fish breaking water on one of our five lakes, quickly transports you back to days of slower living and peaceful scenes. LaPorteans can "have their cake and eat it too." The city is within an hour of every metropolitan advantage, yet snuggled safely and securely in the Northern Indiana countryside.
>
> Make no mistake. LaPorte is a community on the go! But she still remains a friendly, warm, and welcoming place.[4]

The contradictions inherent in the retention of "the charm and easy living" of a past Middle West and "a thriving industrial city" only emerge in discussions of the mass murderess who shattered those "days of slower living and peaceful scenes."

GUNNESSVILLE

Belle Gunness, the lady who put LaPorte metaphorically on the map, moved from Chicago to a farmhouse one mile north of the town limits in the fall of 1901. The forty-eight-acre property on McClung Road looks today much as it did at the turn of the century, although it is now on the town's northern boundary line. Its location, too, has symbolic dimensions, caught as it is between city, town, and rural landscapes on the edges of the community. It remains an icon of the events which catapulted LaPorte, recently called "an archetypical small Midwestern town," with its graciousness and beauty and its clannishness and closeness, into the public eye in 1908.[5] It stands, as it has stood for three-quarters of a century, as a reminder of contradictions.

Carnival blossomed in Belle Gunness's tracks. The excavation of the decomposed bodies of the men who had answered her matrimonial advertisements became a tourist attraction in the spring of 1908. Harry Burr Darling, a reporter for the *LaPorte Argus-Bulletin*, had written, "Hundreds of persons visited the Gunness place today. All roads led to the scene of the holocaust," when only four bodies, presumed to be those of Mrs. Gunness and her children, were found in the basement of the burnt-out farmhouse on April 28. After the men's dismembered bodies were discovered on the grounds a week later, on May 5, Darling's headlines jumped to "Thousands Visit the Place Where Lives Were Taken" (Sunday, 10 May) and "Thousands Re-enact the Scenes of a Sunday Ago" (Sunday, 17 May). This time Darling wrote, "All the roads led to the private burying ground of the arch-murderess of the years . . . and when darkness fell it was roughly estimated that fifteen thousand people had tramped the grounds of the Gunness home." Maxine Ford, a reporter for the *LaPorte Herald-Argus*, echoed Darling's words over sixty years later when she wrote in 1971 that Belle Gunness "made LaPorte a mecca for the curious and for those who prefer real mystery" (26 May 1971).

People who remember these "Gunness Sundays" and others who know family stories about them have mixed feelings about the circuslike atmosphere hovering over their town in those weeks. Oral accounts, although usually simple general statements, reveal a sense of inundation by the outside world. Glen Ott, who was right there, said, "Ya, oh, ya. And they had excursions coming on these railroads here. Boy, they was five, six big trains come in here every day. Had hamburger stands, ice cream stands! And stink. You could smell the place, you know, two blocks away. Them bodies up there in that hogpen, you know." Max Ford, whose parents had seen the excavations, told me that "Chicago went crazy! The newspaper reporters—all the big papers sent their reporters. Excursions went out from Chicago at special reduced rates, and carloads and trainloads of people came into LaPorte. Holidays and Sundays. It was unbelievable that people would bring basket lunches and eat on the grounds while the bodies were being dug up." And Louis Blake, whose wife's family, the Deckers, had once had a farm not far from Mrs. Gunness's, asked me, "Now there's one thing that I don't know whether you've learned, but they ran special trains up from Indianapolis? Yes, they did. The old Lake Erie Railroad. Lake Erie and Western. L, E, and W. Special trains to show them the place out there."[6]

Sightseers didn't all come by excursion train. Many walked from town and surrounding farms. Others came by horse and buggy. Albert Nicholson, whose parent's farm was across McClung Road from the Gunness place, remembered, "Sundays, this road you couldn't hardly walk on it, every fence post had a horse and buggy hitched to it from here to there."[7]

Rural families share stories about property damage which imply an underlying sense of community damage. Dora Rosenow, whose father, William Diesslin, had a farm just south of Mrs. Gunness's, remembered that souvenir hunters "took every little pot and pan and everything they could find out of the ashes . . . I think they carried most of the bricks off." Charles Pahrman, a library custodian considered an expert on the Gunness case in the 1950s, recalled that out-of-towners had cut six to eight feet each of the barb wire fence surrounding the hogpen containing the bodies.[8]

The destruction spread. Megan Backus remembered a family story her grandmother told. The family had had a summer home on Fish Trap Lake near the Gunness farm when the grandmother was a child about the age of Myrtle and Lucy Sorensen, Belle's daughters. "When the thing broke out, reporters came. Reporters came from all over the world . . . They were trampling my mother's flowers. A big, German woman. She was outraged."[9]

John Nepsha, Jr., a retired Allis-Chalmers employee whose parents bought the Gunness property in 1923, talked about the tourists who came for years after the murders to see the site. He said that they came "well, usually on weekends. Up here, when I was a youngster, from all over the United States they came—all different states—they came during the week, too." They looked in the open holes in the lot where the bodies had lain. They took souvenirs, ruining the apple trees in the adjacent orchard by breaking branches in the process. "It didn't bother me, but it bothered my folks. There'd be a lot of people up there, and my Dad'd be up there, you know. Asking him, 'Are you afraid of ghosts or anything?' And my Dad said, 'No, I'm not afraid of ghosts. I'm afraid of the live ones!'"[10]

Accounts of the town's business profits, however, counterbalance the country voices remembering destruction. Hotels, especially the Hotel Teegarden, were jammed with reporters. Restaurants sold chili con carne labeled "Gunness Stew," and bars opened their doors against the rules. Entrepreneurs set up the lemonade and sandwich stands along McClung Road which Maxine Ford and Glen Ott remembered with some amusement. Photographer Henry Koch, who had taken the last known picture of Belle Gunness and her three children, had a Gunness display in his shop on Indiana Avenue and sold copies. Elmore von Winkle hawked picture postcards of the Gunness farmhouse ruins and the farm shed converted into a temporary morgue.[11]

Gene McDonald, whose family were some of the earliest settlers in the county, liked to reminisce about county auctioneer Allison Rodgers Brownlee's most famous sale–the one held on May 29 on the Gunness farm:

> But that sale out there was the craziest thing I ever seen. You know, good God, you know every damn kid skipped school to go out there to that! Not only the boys, either. Al Brownlee was the auctioneer. . . . [Belle Gunness's] butchering stuff was all out in the granary. Then she had, oh, I don't know, I think, four or five cows and some hogs. And she had all kinds of tools. And she had a dog. And she had a beautiful gray team—dapple grays. And Ringling Brothers Circus bought 'em. And give $1800 for 'em, and they would have sold for about $300. . . . Al, he said that was the best sale he ever had.
>
> O, God. I betcha they was five thousand people at that sale. Well, you know, these reporters, all the newspapers was here. Good God,

even the Teegarden home was charging you five or ten dollars to flop on the floor!

But the best of it was old Eb Hill. But he drove a hack out there. He was a colored fella, and he had a kinda fancy outfit they put on him, and they charged you four dollars to go out there, and if you rode on the seat with him, it cost six dollars! Everybody made money out of it.

Gene said, "All these fake shows and that, you know, side shows, they bought pret' near all that stuff." One concern bought Belle's dog, pony, and cart and then put them on the road in a traveling show with Joe Maxson, Belle Gunness's last hired man, who had discovered her farmhouse ablaze the month before. This sideshow attraction confirmed both the carnivalesque aspects of the auction and its profitability.[12]

Mrs. Eldora Burns's father, Daniel Hutson, had helped unearth the bodies from their shallow graves behind the Gunness house. She has told her family for years about the people who streamed up McClung Road all that summer for a chance to walk over the grounds.[13] Elmore van Winkle peddled his postcards among them and, in July, began selling the paperback *The Mrs. Gunness Mystery: A Thrilling Tale of Love, Duplicity, and Crime* for a quarter. He told de la Torre that copies sold like hotcakes. The anonymous author of *The Mrs. Gunness Mystery*, not having the information that Belle's parents had been poor cotters all their lives in Selbu, made up the satisfying tale that Belle's mother had been the queen of a Gypsy camp and her father a giant knife juggler near Trondheim (pp. 9-13). He wrote that Baby Belle had traveled the carnival circuit, watching her father swallow swords and pretend to decapitate her mother in their famed guillotine act. He saw that this gruesome example set up unintended repercussions:

It was during one of these days in fair time that the mother startled Peter, the sword swallower, when she cried to him in excited tones: "Oh, Papa, come, look at baby."

The big showman hastened to the rear of the gypsy tent. There he saw the little girl, prattling merrily to herself and her one childish treasure, a rag doll. She laid the doll across a stick of wood. In her hands she carried one of her father's swords. As the parents reached the spot the baby raised the sword above her head and brought it down with a gurgle of delight across the sawdust neck of the doll of rags. [P. 12]

The author ends the chapter with the rhetorical question: "Was it heredity, or was it childish association with horror that led this child to grow into an ogress, with the lust for letting human blood, the love for rending of bodies limb from limb, and the greed for human heads that caused her to slay and decapitate at least twenty-five children, women and men whose names are known?" (p. 13).

This tale of Belle's youth has had a limited, but lengthy, oral and print circulation in LaPorte. A report surfaced in 1930 that Ray Lamphere, dying of tuberculosis in prison in 1909, had told his nurse, the trusty Harry Myers, much about the life and crimes of his employer Mrs. Gunness. Among other things, "Lamphere said that the woman's maiden name was Paulsen and that she was born in Norway and in early childhood traveled with a circus as a tight rope walker, accompanied by her father, who was a conjuror and a contortionist and who possessed an evil reputation." De la Torre was convinced that the prisoner had had time to read the paperback thriller while he was incarcerated and that it was nothing more than "a mess of undigested newspaper clippings spiced up with red-hot imaginary episodes in thoroughly bad taste." Yet the first page of the LaPorte County Historical Society pamphlet *The Gunness Story*, published in 1964, states that Belle's father was a Gypsy sword swallower and her mother a tightrope walker. Although Maxine Ford thought it one of the most ridiculous stories she'd heard, several residents said that they had always been told that Belle's was a carnival family.[14]

Ray Lamphere's trial flooded LaPorte anew in November of 1908. The courtroom in the county courthouse set on the central green was packed. Spectators spilled out into the corridor and onto the lawn, even though Frank J. Kerwin, an eighteen-year-old employee at LaPorte's carriage works at the time, recalled that a limited number of tickets for seating were distributed. In an unseasonable metaphor, *Argus-Bulletin* reporter Darling compared the trial to a Mayday celebration. Certainly the public response seemed close to the frontier pattern of treating legal trials as the best spectacles for miles around. De la Torre framed her discussion in dramatic terms. "On November 9, 1908," she began, "the curtain went up on one of the most extraordinary courtroom dramas of the century." The second-floor courtroom became the scene of the show, lawyers and judge the supporting actors, the defendant—and the missing murderess—the stars of the drama. The storytelling abilities of the lawyers and their chief witnesses created an image of Belle Gunness that became the region's prime attraction and a profit for LaPorte businesses yet again.[15]

Encoded in these narratives is a certain disjunction between town and country values. Perhaps the problem, too simply expressed, is one between a rising entrepreneurial system, dependent on "cashing in" on an event which brought town businessmen essential clients, and a declining agricultural network, based on intensive labor on the land. The year 1908 falls within the turn-of-the-century shift in values noted by Richard Lingeman in his study *Small Town America*. Town, city, and factory were in a changing relationship as the urbanization of the American landscape progressed. Lingeman quotes Page Smith, who claims that "the older ethic of self denial, of 'character,' of unremitting labor gave way slowly to the cities' values of agressiveness, of enterprise, of deference to riches" (p. 338). The figure of Belle Gunness herself encapsulates these conflicts. She was an immigrant farm woman dependent on her farm products for her own daily needs, for barter with other farm neighbors, and for cash from her town patrons, yet her values were those of the new business ethics.[16]

But people also talked about their experiences when they traveled outside of town themselves and were confronted by strangers asking about their hometown lady killer. These narratives, complements to the ones above, indicate a sense of community notoriety spreading outward across the map. Ruth Andrew Coffeen was one of the last descendants of the Andrew brothers who founded LaPorte. She said, "I remember when I went to college, and when I got my ticket to come back, I asked for it to 'LaPorte, Indiana,' and the ticket agent there said, 'Oh, LaPorte, Indiana! Belle Gunness!' And I said, 'That's right.' And, of course, that was, oh, ten years after it all happened."[17]

Maxine Ford's stories about her mother's conversations with train porters and mailmen when she returned to Memphis, Tennessee in 1913 expand Ruth Coffeen's anecdote about her resigned response to the train agent:

Well, while we were living in Memphis, the train service was marvelous at that time. You know, you could get a train in LaPorte and go into Chicago and then straight to Memphis. And Mother was seated in one of the coaches when one of the porters came up and went to punch her ticket, and he noticed that she was from "Gunnessville." And he was very, very disturbed. It was a black porter. And he knew all about the Gunness case, and he was very disturbed about it. And she said he sort of kept his distance!

And, then, in Memphis, the postal carriers were blacks, and, before they got to your home, they would blow a whistle back then so you'd know your mail was on its way. And Mother was doing fine getting her mail until she went out one day and this black mailman was very tentatively offering her a letter. And he said, "You is from Gunnessville?" And Mother said, "Yes." And he had noticed the postmarks saying "LaPorte, Indiana." And to them it was "Gunnessville." And LaPorte was known as "Gunnessville" all over the country. Some reporter probably gave it the name, you know, and it stuck pretty well. So she said after that he didn't come up to the porch. He would stand out on the sidewalk, and she would go get the mail. It seemed he didn't want to have anything to do with anyone who lived anywhere near the place![18]

The "Gunnessville" label is significant because it points to a conceptual fusion of murderess and town which operated for many of the older residents, at least in their self-definition of community. People have responded to this joint image in quite different ways, however. "I know we can't change history, but why is it always Belle Gunness that is brought to mind when anyone mentions LaPorte? We must have a lot of other things to be known for besides this one incident," Mrs. David Slater asked. When Gene McDonald said, "LaPorte is famous for other things if you want to hang out her dirty wash," he inverted Mrs. Slater's rejection of the woman-town connection. His acceptance included a willingness to speak on any historical topic, no matter how unflattering to the community. Most peoples' attitudes, however, when they care enough to make the choice, lie somewhere in between these two extremes.[19]

When LaPorte celebrated its centennial in 1932, Ruth Andrew was a member of the committee that prepared a festive program of historical skits representing a hundred years of community growth. The Gunness story was *not* included in the centenary production. Its omission corresponds to Yankee City's exclusion of certain historical events from its 1930 tricentennial parade in Warner's study. Both city committees selected for dramatization those events from their available past which symbolized that past perfected and powerful.[20]

Forty years later, in 1972, Ruth and her husband, Robert Coffeen, the son of an Irish mason who had once worked for Belle
Gunness, compiled their history of LaPorte for the local school
system:

> Ruth: But I don't think we told the Belle Gunness story.
> Bob: I don't think we did.
> Ruth: No, we didn't.
> Bob: Not that kind of example. . . . We debated that. We felt it
>   had—for kids that age—it had no place in the sheer history of
>   LaPorte.[21]

The situation is somewhat more complex for LaPorte than for
Yankee City, or for Middletown, however. Yankee City's peak
period of power and glory in maritime shipping was clearly defined
at the end of the eighteenth century, where its tricentennial floats
clustered, while its period of economic decline thereafter was as
clearly known yet not represented. Middletown burst from a small
village to a major manufacturing center in the twentieth century.
Its peak period heralded the progress of the industrial age.
LaPorte's period of economic power has been a fluctuating one and
is not so clearly outlined. Neither is its significant past. Belle Gunness has no place in the small-town *mythos* in the histories above.
But her position is assured in community commemorative events
for many reasons, ironic awareness of the economic benefits which
have accrued and the delight in a good story among them.

DEAR OLD BELLE

Robert Coffeen's twenty-fifth-anniversary article on the Gunness
fire, printed April 28, 1933 in the *Herald-Argus*, was included in
the town's centennial history published in 1938, and initiated the
newspaper tradition of writing annual reports on the case. (They
say in the newspaper edit room that cub reporters get a chance to
try their wings each year on the Gunness case and that new residents, in turn, can read the old story.)

And the historical piece that Ruth Coffeen did not write for the
town's centennial was written in 1947. Variously titled "The Ballad of Blood-Thirsty Belle" and "The Ballad of Belle Gunness," it
has been performed for LaPorte audiences ever since. The ballad

text is based on a conscious parody of a popular honky-tonk number of the 1940s, "Pistol-Packin' Mama," in which the lady gets her man in true Frankie-and-Johnny style. The first stanza of the incremental chorus serves to reinforce the connection between the two women who did their menfolk in:

> Lay that cleaver down, Belle,
> Lay that cleaver down,
> Cleaver-cloutin' Mama
> Lay that cleaver down.

The ballad was sung in a minor key when performed. Ruth Coffeen recalled, "And, of course, in minor key, it *is* gruesome." When asked how audiences reacted, she said, "Oh, they loved it! They laugh. Oh, you can't help but laugh when it's sung that way, you know." Descriptions of three major performances reveal certain incongruities in this laughter. All performances were part of the town's celebratory events: the first recognized the seventieth anniversary of the Women's Literary Society in 1947; the second, an annual revue of the Little Theatre Club in 1957; and the third, the club's golden anniversary in 1975.

When Mrs. Coffeen was asked to arrange the anniversary program for the literary society, she incorporated "The Ballad of Blood-Thirsty Belle," because "it was just too good a chance to miss." The society, founded in 1878, is the oldest cultural organization in town and one of the few survivors of the late-nineteenth-century women's club movements in the United States. Its founding purpose, in line with other study groups' goals, is the mental improvement of its members in history, literature, art, and science. Its high aspirations are matched by the high status of its members. The eight women who founded the society were members of the town's leading families and, in several cases, of its founding families. Subsequent members, often the daughters and granddaughters of the first, have been and are connected through kinship, marriage ties, or professional occupations to the "blue stocking" First Ward. At the time of the performance discussed, membership was exclusive in a double sense—it was extended by invitation only, and it referred to social position. Author, performers, and audience represented the female aristocracy of their community.

The anniversary program, "The Day before Yesterday," included seven skits, each representing one decade of the society's history. The Gunness ballad represented the season of 1907–1908. Ruth Coffeen's introduction keyed the performance to an entertainment mode:

> It was during the spring of this year that event occurred which some people say put LaPorte on the map. Ladies, I refer to none other than the spectacular Belle Gunness murder case. . . . Yes, Belle Gunness, the female Bluebeard, murderess par excellence, with at least fifteen murders to her credit and more to be had for the digging. Ladies, you have had her presented to you in newspapers, in magazines, in books; early this fall you had her on the radio; but never to my knowledge have you had her in music. Ladies, we give you then at this time "The Ballad of Blood-Thirsty Belle," sung by the Gibson Girls Glee Club.

The curtain opened, and the audience saw eight of their number dressed in authentic Gibson girl costumes. The performers sang the ballad with deadpan faces while posed in the elegant upper-class style of the idealized American girl:

> She advertised for a husband
> And advertising pays
> She always knew
> Just what to do
> For she had such killing ways.
>
> Each suitor who came courtin'
> Must first his bride endow
> And then that day
> Without delay
> He fell for her—and how.
>
> Lay that hatchet down, Belle
> Lay that hatchet down
> Hatchet-hackin' Mama
> Lay that hatchet down.

The *Herald-Argus* society page called it "one of the two outstanding hits of the program." The other was a skit depicting a 1920s fashion show.[22]

That Belle Gunness could enter the inner sanctum of this elite women's group and be laughable indicates that their play world was transmuting the murderess and using her in symbolic ways.

Society members' laughter fixed Belle Gunness, the code breaker, next to the Gibson girl, the code maker whom Ernst Earnest has called "the ideal whom many men expected to find someday in the flesh and blood" and who could be an appropriate enough projection of their own social roles.[23] They laughed at the anomalous yoking together of an image that subverted and an image that idealized their class's expectations. Their irony domesticated the murderess by pulling her into their own social milieu, where, at worst, she would tower over men only at social gatherings in artistic representations already fifty years old.

The metamorphosis of the murderess begun in this performance continued in the Little Theatre Club's revue, which was open to the public and, therefore, more representative of the LaPorte community as a whole. "The Ballad of Belle Gunness" played immediately after a selection from the musical *Carousel*. This timing highlighted the carnival world in which the murderess finally and most fully moved. In this presentation, the participants upended social categories and subverted the dramatic and dance forms their club, one of the longest-running theater groups in the country, was pledged to uphold. The singers, barefoot and dressed in black, stared straight ahead, chanting the ballad in a dirgelike monotone and so parodying a Greek chorus. They created the narrative background for the Belle Gunness ballet performed on stage. Belle Gunness was played by Juanita Schnable, a local hairdresser said to be built a bit like the hefty murderess, while Andrew Helgelien, Gunness's last victim, was played by John Hacker, a small man who was a clerk in the local post office.

Oral histories of the performance focus on one crucial scene. The chorus was singing this stanza:

> When Andrew Helgelien came,
> His check he first cashed in
> And then that night
> She caught him right
> And he was soon bashed in.

Juanita, as Belle, had just exited stage rear. John, as Andrew, bringing a little bouquet of flowers, knocked at the farmhouse door. As he handed over the bouquet, Belle's arm shot from the wings and jerked him up and out so that his body became horizontal with the stage floor as he was pulled through the air. Cast, audience, and stage crew were amazed at the acrobatic feat that turned the incongruity of body sizes into both a visual metaphor of power and a slapstick routine.

The final scene is marked by these stanzas:

> When Andrew's brother Asa [Asle]
> Had written to inquire
> She lost her head
> And it is said
> She set the place on fire.
>
> They couldn't find a head
> They couldn't find a skull
> So people said
> Perhaps instead
> She wasn't dead at all.

Belle moved slowly across the stage into the darkness of the wings, holding a severed head under her arm. The head, ostensibly Belle's own, was immediately recognized by the audience as one belonging to Juanita's beauty shop mannikin. This recognition juxtaposed the grotesque world of Belle Gunness's violence with the comfortable world of Juanita's beauty salon. The murderess had become "Dear Old Belle" at long last.

When Juanita Schnable said that she had to choreograph the whole production herself because none of the other theater club members knew what to do, Maxine Ford, one of the chorus, quipped, "Well, they'd never seen Belle dance!" Audiences were given the chance to see her dance in successive performances, for the same cast performed the ballet for the club's fiftieth anniversary and for several LaPorte County Historical Society meetings, as well.[24]

"The Ballad of Belle Gunness" turned a woman's violence into a caper and the woman herself into a living curiosity exhibited in a show. Steve James told me that hers is a "story just everybody seems to know. We keep it around as a national attraction. Even her name, you know, 'Belle' Gunness, implies a circus attraction. You know how circus sideshows are—'How strong is the strong man? How fat is the fat lady?' And here she was, a murderer, a freak." Stewart Holbrook had much the same conception when he wrote that "Belle Gunness lives on in that misty, unmapped half-world that Americans have made and lovingly preserve for certain of their folk villains. Indeed, I fully expected to see Belle pop up at Chicago's Century of Progress World's Fair in 1933, complete with cleavers and a supply of quicklime. . . ." He was disappointed, but, had he been alive and in LaPorte for the local preparations for the United States Bicentennial in 1975, he would certainly have appreciated Maxine Ford's special addition to the festivities.[25]

As a member of the town's Bicentennial committee to select an appropriate statue for the Independence Plaza then being constructed behind the present courthouse, Maxine Ford suggested a bust of Belle Gunness, because "certainly, she brought more fame to the city than anyone before or since!" Although the committee selected a statue of a Potawatomi chief breaking his bow in a sign of peace, the suggestion for a Belle Gunness statue spread through the service club communication network—the Kiwanis, the Elks, and the Lions clubs. Maxine's sense of the comic was shared by her immediate audience and by every subsequent teller and listener of the anecdote, many of them prominent citizens. The humor in the situation grew out of the recognition of the tension created by joining incongruous elements on several levels. The double play on the word "bust" connected the austere image of civic statuary with the sensual image of Belle's breasts, which were estimated at an ample forty-seven inches. It also connected the Bicentennial themes of "life, liberty, and the pursuit of happiness" with the grotesqueness of a woman who butchered immigrants instead of harboring them, a perverse Statue of Liberty indeed to represent the community.[26]

Through these dramatic juxtapositions of opposites, community members, like the cult members in sacred ritual observed by Mary Douglas, seemed able "to turn round and confront the categories on which their whole society has been built up and to recognize them for the fictive, man-made creations that they are."[27] Belle Gunness, finally the comic monster, reminds townspeople of the social contradictions with which they live. The town saying "Belle Gunness put us on the map" has reached a certain proverbial status, perhaps because it embodies a range of attitudes towards the issue of modernization underlying the Gunness phenomenon. For the entrepreneurial class presented here, "Dear Old Belle" is an ironic tourist attraction; for other community members, however, she is simply a monster who signals the demise of older values.

† 2 †

THE MURDER FARM

Most people living in LaPorte can point out the property on McClung Road, still marked by a double row of dark-green cedars, that once held the mystery of Belle Gunness. Few, however, know the history of the place prior to her ownership. A reading of the abstract of the property, which outlines transactions from the original land purchase by treaty from the Potawatomi Nation in 1826 to the most recent legal proceedings of the present owners, shows at least thirteen holders prior to its purchase by Mrs. Gunness, still the Widow Sorensen, in November of 1901.[1]

THE GENEALOGY OF THE HOUSE

The anonymous author of the 1908 *The Mrs. Gunness Mystery* selected four of the previous owners to suggest the somber precedents for the "Murder Farm." The disastrous lineage included the farmer who built the home on the grounds, a madam who poisoned herself over a love affair, two brothers who died suddenly, and a head of household who hanged himself from his bedpost and subsequently haunted the area (pp. 40–42). This list of horrors, although it does not differentiate sudden death, suicides, or hauntings from the Gunness murders, does form a sort of genealogy of evil, placing events in an evaluative framework.[2]

The genealogies of two LaPorte historians, both considered experts in the Gunness case, go a step further. Each pares the house's family tree down to the relationships shared by the successive women who lived on the property. Their telescoped histories focus on the ladies who were literally and metaphorically on the edge of town. Each historian perceives these unruly women, caught in the liminal space of deviancy, in quite different ways.

Gene's Story

Gene McDonald was born in 1890 to a family who had settled in LaPorte and Porter counties before the town of LaPorte was plotted. He had ample opportunity to learn about county history. He traveled as a young boy with his uncle, "a horse doctor." They went from farm to farm to check on the animals and heard and passed on stories of current interest as they did so. "I used to get around a lot with him when I was a kid. If I'd a wrote all that stuff down! You know, every damn place we'd go, the roosters always hid! They'd always have some stories to tell about some neighbors, this and that." Later, as a railroad yard worker, then a fireman on the Michigan Central Railroad, Gene picked up tales on his regular runs from Michigan City to points in Michigan.

Gene sat almost every afternoon in the front room of the Historical Society Museum, reminiscing with staff and visitors who asked about local history. Conversations on Mayme Jonas's front porch, in whose home he boarded before his death in 1979, and at the Salvation Army Citadel, where he participated in the hot lunch program for senior citizens, often revolved around LaPorte lore. And Gene often had the last word.

Eighteen years old at the time of the Gunness murders, he watched the bodies unearthed and the auction progress at the McClung Road site. He participated in many discussions, and just as many arguments, about the property. A collation of his observations on the Gunness home, which he said always "had a sordid reputation," indicates how the house, the women who lived in it, and the town itself were delicately intertwined.[3] He said, "The house. Well, that was built [in 1846] for Harriet Holcomb, the daughter of one of the founders of LaPorte, John Walker. And he built these four mansions. . . . All the Walker mansions was made out of brick. And they all had marble furnaces." Gene commented on the Holcomb mansion in particular. "Ah, that was a wonderful house. It have five fireplaces with marble mantles and mirrors all over." The four brick mansions Walker built for each of his children—William J. Walker, LaPorte's first mayor, among them—showed not only the solidity of the Walker family ties but also the cohesiveness of the early community's political organization. The houses, foursquare, functioned as the cornerstones of the pioneer settlement. Perhaps Gene shared with Sherwood Anderson the idea that the roof of home was a metaphor of the small community.[4]

Gene said that the Holcombs, however, had "trouble in the Civil War." They moved to King's County, New York in 1864 because they were Southern sympathizers in a Union town. And the house stood empty. Gene, a Civil War buff who still mourned the 1,500 men LaPorte County had lost and whose father and four uncles had fought on the Union side, must have seen this move as disruptive on several levels. The abandoned Holcomb house was a chink out of the earlier family and community solidarity, and it represented the ideological differences splitting families and towns during the war between the states.

The chink was widened when Mattie Altic, a madam from Chicago whose "two big, biggest friends was Hinky-dink and Bathhouse John,"[5] purchased the property in 1892 (actually twenty-eight years and six owners later) and turned the place into "a sporting house." One of Gene's favorite stories was how he met Mattie Altic once when he went to her house to buy some horses with his uncle:

> I can remember her as a kid, you know. She had the fanciest driving horses. My uncle bought a couple. I was there once, and she give me a sack of candy. It was good candy. I'd never eaten it. It was too damn rich. It kinda made me sick afterwards. But she used to drive these fancy horses on a—well, it was a surrey that—you seen 'em with the fringe on top? Well, she used to drive it with them girls downtown, and she always had white lines.
>
> I say Mattie Altic had a barn to keep them horses, fancy barn, too. They had, the stalls in there was all fixed up so-and-so. Then she had a fancy hack that they met the trains. And that had curtains so they couldn't see who was going there.
>
> But you know what I used to laugh about? When she come to town, she'd bring two or three of them girls, and she'd go into the stores like

Davidson and Porter. They [the store clerks] would go out of the rule to fawn on her, to wait on them. 'Course they bought. But she had the biggest ostrich plume I ever seen! I can remember. As a kid, you know, she was a great curiosity to us.

She had the most beautiful marble, in her parlor there or whatever you want to call it, entertaining room. And she had a bar in there too! And across the road she had a kind of park and a boat landing where they went out on Fish Trap. It was a swell place. Real swell.

Mattie Altic and her girls, demimondaines from the big city, brought a bit of Chicago's Gold Coast to LaPorte. As we've seen from the preceding chapter, this influx found a mixed response in the small town. Prostitutes in the Gilded Age, "soiled doves" that they were, gave McClung Road a poor reputation up to the First World War. Their numerous lovers coming in on the interurban and their conspicuous consumption symbolized their reversal of the town's professed values of premarital chastity, monogamy, and thriftiness, as Lingeman notes (pp. 267–68). Yet their rich living fascinated admiring children and encouraged small-town merchants to bend the rules for their good business.

Gene remembers that Mattie was tall and full-blown but not fat. Yet her high living proved too much for her. She dropped dead of a heart attack at a relatively early age. "But I can remember her funeral," he said. "They had about thirty hacks, them people come from Chicago. Alf Earle, over in Michigan City, had the funeral. He had a wonderful turnout. She's buried out in Pine Lake [Cemetery]."

And, if Mattie was bad but elegant in Gene's estimation, Belle Gunness was only bad. The murderess, who had bought the Altic place because "nobody wanted it and it was cheap" (actually eight years and four owners later), should have stayed in Chicago, as far as he was concerned. The house had been "in good shape yet when she got it," but she immediately insured the fancy carriage house and the boat pavilion and burnt them up for the insurance money. "Well, she didn't have no use for that. She just had a barn. She just had cows, work horses." For Gene, the acts of arson foreshadow Mrs. Gunness's burning of her farmhouse several years later, for he was convinced that "she knew all the ropes" and planned her escape in a way with which she was all too familiar.

Belle's clientele was not Mattie's Chicago high society but hardy immigrant farmers. "She had quite a few Norwegians come from Minnesota. But most of them that she butchered were all Norwegians." Her relations with these men were not only illicit but also murderous, the ultimate reversal of the ideal bond between men and women! Her relationship with store clerks in town was neither as cordial nor as profitable as Mattie's had been. "You know, Old Belle was kind of a keptomaniac [sic]. She used to pick stuff up around, around sales. Ya. Everybody knew that. Hell, everybody was scared of her!"

And her behavior at public sales was decidedly déclassé. "But I can remember though she used to go around to public sales. All of 'em. And she always—up on her stocking, up here [Gene placed his hands on his upper inner thigh], she always had a roll of bills, and when she come to pay she always paid cash. She'd draw her dress up and pull her stocking down and get it. To us kids, you know, that was interesting." And, in place of Mattie's elegant ostrich plume, Gene recalled Belle, who topped six feet and weighed 250 pounds, sporting her own full face, "as red as a tomato." Added to her destruction of property, Mrs. Gunness's stealing from local stores and at public auctions finally marked the disintegration of community.

Martin's Story

Martin Barlag was born in 1910, three years before his father came to LaPorte to work at the Advance-Rumely Company. A retired employee of Allis-Chalmers, he has developed an interest in local history which has a more literary base than Gene McDonald's experiential focus. His basement library is filled with bound stacks of old newspapers, city directories, historical magazines, and well-labeled notebooks filled with clippings, legal material, and date notations. One of these notebooks, labeled *Gunness-Crimes*, confirms the claim that he has "the largest collection of Belle Gunness material in the world" in private hands.

He depicted the house in Mattie's day in a much more sinister light than Gene had.[6] His genealogy outlines a pervasive sense of community fragmentation rather than a progressive deterioration; it forges strong links between the house of prostitution and the house of murder. "I have a little story about the place itself," he began. "Prior to Gunness living there, it was called 'the Farm.'

There were iron bars on the windows when it was used as 'the Farm,' and, of course, they remained there when Mrs. Gunness was there." Martin said that the bars had served a double purpose when Madam Altic was in charge. "Some of the girls were brought there as white slaves and kept there against their will, see." The bars kept them *in*. "And also some of these local gay blades, you know, imbibed too much and got out there, and they would attempt to break in and so on." And the bars kept them *out*, unless they, too, had the funds to be admitted at the front door with the wealthy Chicago gentlemen.

The bars presumably had a twofold purpose when Mrs. Gunness ran her "Murder Farm," as well. The unlucky men who had answered her matrimonial advertisements stayed *in* until she transferred them, in pieces, to her hogpen, although several are said to have made their escape before it was too late. And the LaPorte community was kept *out* of the house and off the grounds so that she could continue her criminal activities.

Martin used a prison metaphor to connect Mattie's "man trap" (a contemporary figurative term for a house of prostitution) with Belle's literal man trap and to separate them both from ordered family and community life. His account of community traditions about the house's evil influences tangibly reinforces the connections perceived:

> Well, this version I've heard from a number of people. That the house of prostitution that it had been prior to Mrs. Gunness buying the place, that the evil of those days persisted in that site. Just as though, you know, some people believe in the actual, physical impersonation of the Devil right there, see. And that that site was so impregnated with evil that it brought all the other effects on Mrs. Gunness to being, see.

Martin glossed the tradition by saying, "That's, you might say, a superstitious slant on it." He discredited the occult explanation for Belle Gunness's murders, because he knew that she had been implicated in killing her first husband, Mads Sorensen, in Chicago in 1900, long before she had come under the influence of the house on McClung Road.

He did admit, however, that "there is something about this association of evil breeding evil because, when you speak of this

Mattie Altic, you see how she and her sister feuded and attempted to dispose of one another, see." He attributed Mattie's sudden death not to a romantic suicide or to a heart attack but to sororicide. "Mattie took her [her sister Eva Ruppert, who ran a similar house of prostitution in South Bend] to court, saying she was trying to poison her—and I guess she succeeded!" For Martin, the Gilded Age is considerably tarnished. Chicago's vice rings, prostitution, white slave trade, and feuding women were apt examples for the "Mistress of Murder Hill."

Martin's account echoes those of the white-slave tracts which flourished in the first decades of the twentieth century, what Mark Connelly calls the "spicy cultural counterpart to the stuffy vice commission reports." In his *The Response to Prostitution in the Progressive Era*, Connelly analyzes the underlying meanings of the white-slave hysteria hitting the United States in those years. He finds that the plots of these tracts were surprisingly similar: a chaste country girl goes to the city and falls victim to a vice ring which forces her into a life of prostitution. He sees that the plots parallel two real anxieties—concern about the migration of rural women to the cities, and concern about the existence of urban red-light districts.[7]

In the story Martin tells, of course, the reverse movement—and the reverse anxiety—is revealed. Mattie Altic brought Chicago's vice district and white slaves *to* LaPorte. And Belle Gunness performed a further reversal. As an immigrant (immigrants were often seen as the leaders of vice rings in these white-slave tracts), she brought immigrant men to LaPorte. The influx of immigrants was a concern of American natives throughout this period and for successive periods thereafter.

Connelly suggests that the symbolic import of these tracts, and of the whole response to prostitution in this era, is related to anxieties produced by the social and cultural changes occurring at the turn of the century. His analysis of prostitution narratives as a master symbol parallels the hypothesis being developed here. He writes, "During the tumultuous years between the closing of the landed frontier in 1890 and the end of World War I, the United States was transformed from a predominantly rural-minded, de-centralized, principally Anglo-Saxon, production-oriented, and morally absolutist society to a predominantly urban, centralized,

multi-ethnic, consumption-oriented, secular and relativist society."
When he states that "this transformation in American society is
generally regarded as forward-looking and modernizing" but that
it was "accompanied, however, by contrapuntal themes of tension,
anxiety and fear," he touches on the contradictory stances we have
been exploring in a medium-sized city's response to a mass
murderess.[8]

The Skeleton in the Closet

As every family tree has its illegitimate branches, so Belle Gunness's brick house had a shadowy relation with a wooden shack on
Pulaski Street near the New York Central railroad crossing. This
small shack was the home of Elizabeth Smith, a black woman
whose husband had come to LaPorte soon after the Civil War to
work on the railroad. She lived on "the Levee" on the south shore
of Clear Lake at the turn of the century, within a marginal community in the First Ward that was tolerated by the rest of the
town. Martin Barlag said that the Levee, whose very name con-
nects it to the famous First Ward vice district in Chicago, "was a
story in itself. All the strange characters of the town used to con-
gregate there." There was the Queen of the Levee and its King,
who had once stolen a train. There was LaPorte's famous fat lady,
who went on the sideshow circuit, and a tightrope walker with one
leg. There were black migrant and Irish immigrant shanties
spread throughout the area.

Martin commented that "Nigger Liz was a strange character, to
say the least. She was a weird character. And when I say weird, I
mean weird! They used to call it 'Paradise Row' out there. Nigger
Liz and all her Irish neighbors would have feuds, be in court, accused of assault and battery." Gene McDonald remembered that
the area was called "Clabber Alley," because those same Irish
neighbors ate clabbered cream and potatoes.

Narratives about Elizabeth Smith's early life indicate that she
was always on the far side of the law. Maxine Ford, whose father,
Taylor Ray, had been a deputy sheriff and then a mayor of
LaPorte, heard that "at one time, apparently, she was a very, very
attractive young girl and the mistress of a number of professional
men, very prominent professional men, in the town. And had, it
was rumored, a daughter by a local attorney." Charles Cochrane

had heard the same rumor: "Nigger Liz was a powerful woman. She was the 'black sheep' of the family, had a half-white daughter by a prominent man in LaPorte. Once she went to his office on the second floor of a building on Main Street [now Lincoln Way] and had a dispute with him. Her winning agrument was to hold him out the window by his feet!"

By the time Belle Gunness and Elizabeth Smith knew each other, Liz had become very strange. Maxine Ford remembered that "she had no means of livelihood except sort of odd jobs, as I remember. And then she got into that syndrome of stacking newspapers around the rooms [of her home], which is something that often a recluse will do." Several people remember running past her place as children, filled with terror, but that she was kind to them. Glen Ott, whose family lived on Park Street just west of Pulaski Street at the time, had a typical encounter. Liz was on the way back from the bottling works with a case of beer. He continued:

> And she just got there to the crossing, and the bottom fell out of her sack. And the bottles rolled all over, see. And she said [making his voice guttural], "Boy, help me pick them up." She was awful, you know, gruff-talking. And, so, I was scared to death. I helped her pick 'em up all right.
>
> But, ever after that, every time I'd come past her house, she was always setting on her front porch, she'd speak to me and say hello. Ya, she was a big nigger.

Liz's shack and Belle's fine house were associated in several different ways. Ray Lamphere, the hired man accused of firing the Gunness home, was believed to be both women's lover and to spend alternate nights in each house. Martha Alderfer, sister of Mrs. Gunness's last hired man, Joe Maxson, recalled that whenever Belle had Ray arrested for trespassing on her property after she had dismissed him from her employment in February 1908, Mrs. Smith would pay his fine. And Mrs. Gunness would do the same when Liz had similar warrants issued for his arrest.[9]

In fact, Ray Lamphere told his defense attorney, Wirt Worden, that he could not have set the fire at Mrs. Gunness's in the early morning of April 28 because he had been at Mrs. Smith's at the time. Since a white man's being with a black woman was frowned upon, as Gene McDonald put it, and because blacks were not allowed to take the witness stand at the time, Elizabeth Smith did not testify in Ray's behalf at the November trial.[10] This omission seemed inexcusable to people in LaPorte as the years passed, for those who knew her felt that she could have unlocked many secrets which still remain mysteries.

Older residents remember that the two women often exchanged visits. For Mrs. Almetta Hay, their relationship was one of mistress to servant. "Liz always used to go out to Belle Gunness's and help her. She worked out there as a hired hand." For George Heusi, whose grandmother lived just a few blocks from Liz, the relationship was on more of an equal footing. "Liz went out to the Gunness place all the time. They were good friends. She knew more about it than people thought." And for Martha Alderfer, Liz ultimately became Mrs. Gunness's savior. Isaiah Alderfer, Martha's husband, had delivered a load of coal to Liz's place in late April, several days after the Gunness fire. He had had to climb over a pile of rags as high as a wall to make the delivery. He had seen two plates on the table and two women eating. Liz had shouted at him, "Dump the coal and get out!" He had been certain that it was Mrs. Gunness sitting there with her in the dark.[11]

Elizabeth Smith told attorney Worden that she would tell him the true story before she died. As Maxine Ford tells it, "She told Wirt that when she felt she was dying, she would call him and tell him everything she knew about the case. And, unfortunately, when word came that she was dying and wanted to see him, Wirt was on a hunting trip (I think out West), and at that time, communications just weren't that good. And, although they tried to track him down, they never could find him." And, as a result, the secrets died with her in 1916.[12]

When A. J. Harness was hired to clean out Liz's shack after her death, he had his work cut out for him. He found tons and tons of rubbish; the floor was covered several feet deep with papers, tin cans, chairs, iron, and rags, "filth and dirt of every kind and description." His greatest find, a human skull tucked between two mattresses, caused a major controversy in the town. One faction felt that this skull was the one belonging to the decapitated body found in the Gunness farmhouse eight years before. An *Argus-Bulletin* article connected the revival of rumors about the Gunness case to Chicago reporters' hopes of stirring up "a big Gunness sensation," once again putting LaPorte on the map.

Another faction accepted the evidence of Mrs. Smith's black

neighbors that Liz had had the skull for years before she met Belle and had used it in various voodoo practices. A local reporter sent out to cover the find talked to a neighbor, who told him, "She used that skull to conjure with. My mother, she's dead now, but she often told me about how she see her sitting up at night with the light shining through the holes in the skull and Nigger Liz she sit and read to it out of the Bible." Some felt that Liz needed a murderer's skull to cure her own abdominal ailments; others felt that the head, carved with names and initials, was used in magical attempts to kill various police officers and the city marshal whom she hated.[13]

There is some evidence that LaPorte officials preferred the occult explanation to the one reviving the Gunness case. The first was easier to dismiss than the second. At any rate, Liz's refuse-filled shack, her extralegal activities with prominent men, police and lawyers included, and her witchcraft practices placed her as a deviant woman at the town's center.

The genealogies, in selectively charting the lives of women who were seen as town curiosities, said something about the town itself. Those stories relating Belle Gunness to Harriet Holcomb and Mattie Altic kept disorder at bay on the fringes of the community. Those connecting the murderess to Elizabeth Smith, however, moved the disorder inward to the fringe elements within the heart of the community. The stories, as the folk art of the town's oral historians, outlined the changes that LaPorte experienced in just those watershed years between 1890 and 1920. They used the women and their houses as what Mary Douglas would call "natural symbols" for expressing conflicting attitudes towards these changes.[14] Mattie Altic, representing big-city elegance and vice, and Elizabeth Smith, representing black-migrant sensuality and occultism, were enticing, yet disturbing, alternatives to the community's structure. Their connection to Belle Gunness, however, who consistently took one more step beyond the pale, suggests that breaking social boundaries too quickly can be disastrous. The message in these lineages is a warning to hold to values of the past century and to test the new most carefully.

GOOD FENCES MAKE GOOD NEIGHBORS

The narrator in Robert Frost's poem "Mending Wall" cannot explain why he and his neighbor continue to repair the dry-stone fence between their properties when

> He is all pine and I am apple orchard.
> My apple trees will never get across
> And eat the cones under his pines, I tell him.

His neighbor's habitual response—the proverb "Good fences make good neighbors"—provokes him to ask, *"Why* do they make good neighbors? Isn't it/ Where there are cows?"[15]

Pine and apple trees actually do figure in residents' statements about Mrs. Gunness's relations with her neighbors. Madeline Kinney, former curator of the Historical Society Museum, gave these directions for recognizing the property on McClung Road: "You'll see a row of trees. You see, she didn't want people to see what she did. She shielded it with a row of pine trees." Gene McDonald summed up the relationship: "She never associated. The kids never stole her apples!"[16] The Gunness trees are not neutral—they function as signs of Belle Gunness's secretiveness and alienation. They show her violation of the small-town codes of open hospitality between neighbors, as Lingeman notes (p. 291).

But, for Mrs. Gunness's immediate neighbors on McClung Road, the incident of the cows epitomizes her unneighborliness. All the farm families raised some crops and livestock, principally for subsistence, although dairy products, poultry, and some produce were sold in town. The acreage of each farm was not large, so cattle were taken to graze along the road. Children often had this task. It was their duty to watch the cattle morning and evening, before and after school, to make sure that none strayed into the fenced-in areas on each farm which protected the growing and stored crops. Neighbors shared these fences in common and were jointly responsible for their maintenance.

William Diesslin had the ill luck to be Mrs. Gunness's neighbor and to share a common fence between their properties. His youngest daughter, Dora Rosenow, recalled, "Well, I tell you this woman kept you away from her. She was very hard to get along with. She had a farm, and all the fences she'd let go, so her cattle

would go in your field. Well, you know, that causes hard feelings."
Mrs. Rosenow went on to stress the fact that "*no* one was a friend
of hers. And she'd *always* keep you kinda so you didn't want to
have nothing to do with her. *All* the neighbors, not just us."[17]

One of those neighbors, Mrs. Swan Nicholson, said that she was
the only neighbor Mrs. Gunness had anything to do with. Her son
Albert, however, said that Mrs. Gunness had been friendly with
the neighbors in her first years in the neighborhood but quarreled
with all the families, and nobody went there for about four years
before the fire (1904–1908). As a case in point, he cited a specific
incident between Mrs. Gunness and William Diesslin which has
entered family and local traditions.

The Story of the Cows

ALBERT'S VERSION

> William Diesslin had corn right across road [from us]. [Belle] had
> two heifer calves. He had fixed up fence, she'd tear fence down again.
> Let them in. Had no feed for them. Finally he drove them into his
> barn and sent a kid up to notify her. She came down. He demanded
> pay, stood in front of the barn door and said she had to pay damages.
> She pulled out a butcher knife. "Damn you, you get away from that
> door or I'll kill you right there!" This was in the fall [probably of
> 1904]. *Diesslin was afraid of her.*[18]

George Heusi, William Diesslin's nephew, remembered his uncle's telling the story somewhat differently.

GEORGE'S VERSION

> Well, his cows got out first. She drove them into her yard and
> locked them up. Took out a .45 revolver and said, "You can't have
> them until you pay fifty dollars for damages." And there wasn't even
> any damages.
> Then *her* cows got out, and he took them in and wouldn't let *her*
> have them until she paid fifty dollars! *He sure made her pay it back!*[19]

The differences in Albert's and George's stories may be due to
differences in kinship ties. Albert, a nonrelative, recalled William
Diesslin's fear. His version of the neighbors' interaction is condensed and monoepisodic, culminating in Mrs. Gunness's butcher

knife. The shape of his story is as one-sided as the murderess's overreaction which warranted her neighbor's justifiable qualms. George, a relative, highlighted his uncle's one-upmanship. His version expresses the interaction in two parallel episodes which outline the reciprocal nature of the exchange, its "an eye for an eye and a tooth for a tooth" quality.

A look at his daughter Dora's accounts of her father's meeting with Belle, however, shows that kin/not-kin categories as an explanation for variation in the stories is too simple an answer. Something else is emerging as this story is told and retold.

DORA'S VERSIONS

You'd go down and you'd tell her: "Now, either fix your fences or pay for your cattle or shut them up." Which we finally did. One time my father locked them in the barnyard, and she come down, and we had a padlock on the gate, and she said, "I want my cattle." And he said, "Well, if you give me a dollar, then you can have them." So, she sent this hired girl, Jennie. She says, "Jennie, go home and get a dollar." And she come down here with the dollar, and she handed it to him, and he took off the padlock, and he—and the chain—and he said, "This ought to be around your neck up in that tree!" *And, you know, he hated her that bad!* And she just turned as white as a sheet, took her cattle, and went home.

So, then, she watched. We used to have to watch the cows along the road, you know, let them eat along the road to pasture. And we were coming home from school one night. We seen [our cattle] were out there, and, when they got to her house, she opened the gate and run them all in.

So she says to my father, "Now, when you give me a dollar, you can have them!" And my Dad said, "But you run them in here off the road!" She said, "I don't care." My Dad was going to unhook the gate, and she says to this Jennie, she says, "Jennie, go in and get the revolver." And the girl did. And so he had to pay her a dollar! *That's the kind of neighbor she was.*[20]

In Dora's story, the neighbors' confrontation occurs in parallel episodes which are similar to George's although the actions are in reverse order and are not completely reciprocal. Here, the Diesslin cows' coming on the Gunness property is a function of Belle's overreaction and not Diesslin's neglect. It is her attempt at "getting even" which creates an imbalance in the neighbors' relationship.

The injustice is literally and metaphorically on her side of the fence and is reflected in the structure of the narrative. Diesslin is not afraid of Belle, but neither is he an equal partner in the feuding. Mrs. Gunness overstepped the boundaries of civility, and he could not follow, being a civil man. Yet he did go so far as to verbally wish her hanging from his apple tree. He symbolically reciprocated.

Dora's gloss on the second episode—"That's the kind of neighbor she was!"—shifts the focus away from her father and towards the mass murderess. In another version of "the story of the cows," Dora emphasizes Mrs. Gunness's overreaction to the incident, which brings this account close to Albert's in tone:

> Well, that was funny. We were coming home from school, and we saw that our cows were going down the railroad crossing. And we saw that lady come out and head 'em off and run 'em in her yard. We run in and told our Dad about it—that Old Lady Gunness took our cows in her yard. So he says, "I'll go down and get 'em."
>
> So he went to get them. And she said, "No, not until you pay me a dollar." She said, "Your cows are trespassing." So he said, "No, you herded them in here!" And she says, "Not until you pay a dollar."
>
> So he went to open the gate and let them out, and she hit him with a horsewhip and says, "Don't touch that gate." And she said to her stepdaughter, the working girl, "Jennie, go in and get the gun." And the girl went in and got the gun. She says, "Don't you touch that gate 'til you pay me a dollar." And he had to pay her a dollar. And that's the way it goes. That's exactly the way it goes.[21]

When Dora's grandson Ronnie Rosenow asked her, "Was she serious?" Dora added a condensed episode: "Well, her cows came down first. That's what started it. Her cows were in *our* fields. Not on the road."

RONNIE'S ALTERNATIVE VERSIONS

> The cow went over into his pasture. Ya. In Grandpa Diesslin's pasture. So he put a lock and chain on the gate. And [Mrs. Gunness] didn't want to pay to get the cow back, so she said to one of her daughters to go get the gun. She had a pistol, I guess it was. In the house. The daughter started to go away, and he said, "Stop! I'll let you have them for free!" *Cause he knew that she really would have got, gotten the gun out 'cause they weren't too good of friends. Grandma said that they were really enemies.*

And, then awhile after that, *his* cow got over there, so he had to pay to get it out!

It might have been that his went in there first and then he had to pay to get it back. And then [Belle Gunness's cow] went over in his [field], and she wouldn't pay to get it back. *Or something like that. I can't remember.*[22]

Ronnie's confusion about how the story happened is understandable. His uncertainty about the progression of events is more than memory failure, however. His alternate renditions, in comparison with the other versions coming from William Diesslin's first-hand account of his confrontation with the murderess, incorporate all the possibilities of the incident. Ronnie's stories move from history as irreversible time to myth as reversible time. Whose cows initiated the action, which was antecedent and which was consequent act, is not as important as the symbolic statement of the relationship between the neighbors: "They were really enemies."

Ronnie's reversible narrative has loosened the symbolic model from the event itself. Other neighbors, experiencing similar difficulties with Mrs. Gunness, have applied the model to other events similarly perceived. Albert Nicholson's 1952 account of his father's altercation with his neighbor over her wandering pigs has much the same formal structure and much the same inverted message about neighborliness.

The Story of the Pigs

[Belle] had a sow and pigs, let them out. They'd get into the corn. My father drove them home three or four times. Here'd come that sow and pigs again, growed quite big by this time. Pa, he began to cuss. I said, "Let's shut 'em up." The four of us [Albert, his younger brother John, his father, Swan, and his mother] shooed them pigs into our pigpen, and Mrs. Gunness stood on the hill and watched us. (You could see up there then, not so many trees.)

We hitched up my horse and buggy [to reach the constable to put in a complaint], but, while we were hitching, she drove past in her horse and buggy. The law was a dollar a head [for damages]. Constable Walker went up and told her she had to pay, eleven dollars. She gave him the money. Dad drove them back in on their place. We never saw them pigs again.

Next day, Monday, Mother went uptown, met Mrs. Gunness.

"That's all Mr. Nicholson has been trying to do all these years is get my money. Well, now he's got it. I don't want nothing more to do with any of you." *She kept her word, never came here, we never went there.*[23]

The family sagas of Belle Gunness's straying livestock become metaphors of the murderess as boundary breaker. Her broken fences and destructive cows and pigs contain the messages, once again through inversion, of what it was to be a good neighbor in a community that still valued the shared responsibility for private lands and property, although those communal patterns were already shifting under urban influences. Her campaign of alienation was so effective that neither William Diesslin nor Swan Nicholson went to her home that Tuesday morning of April 28, 1908 to help douse the fire. Dora remembered:

> The morning that the house burnt was the last day of school, the 28th of April, and we always had a picnic. And, 'course, my mother woke up and was going—('course, they didn't have a bathroom then, at that time, they had an outside toilet). She woke up and she looked out the window, and she said to my dad, "Looks like a fire up at the old lady's."
> And he said, "Aw, c'mon to bed. She's probably got the house insured good, and she's going to burn it up now." *And he wouldn't even get up and look*. And, 'course, my mother went back to bed and worried about it, but she never got up to look what time it was or anything.
> And, then, time for us kids to get up, our Dad hollered up, "Time to get up! C'mon down, the old lady burnt her house up last night." *And, you know, he didn't even go up to the house to see what happened.* And, of course, the police came out, then we found out that the house had burnt up and, supposedly, the whole family, see.[24]

And Albert remembered:

> When the fire started, Mother, a light sleeper, woke in the morning, getting daylight, asked, "How come the sun is coming up on this side of the house?" Ma and John wanted to go up, but Pa says, "You stay away, she's mad at us, you could get the blame for starting it."[25]

These two remarkably similar accounts are also models of Belle Gunness's disintegrative power. Under other circumstances, these two men would have joined other farmers in harvesting crops, in raising barns, or in putting out fires—the way of country neighbors even at the turn of the century. They would have heeded their

wives' first impulses to give aid. As it was, Belle Gunness's abuse
of a neighbor's rights had caused a corresponding atrophy of her
neighbors' obligations. The rules for the social relationships within
the rural community had been broken with the fences. The stories,
which foreshadow Mrs. Gunness's greatest asocial acts, her murders, also justify her neighbors' anger and their ignorance of her
activities. The Diesslin and Nicholson families' folk art points to a
transition from the ideal of cooperation and mutual helpfulness
embodied in communal labor to that of a rugged individualism,
which Page Smith sees as "not a product of the towns and farms
but rather of the depersonalized life of the cities."[26]

When Arthur J. Vidich and Joseph Bensman conducted their
controversial study of "Springdale," a rural community in upstate
New York coping with mass society, they found that "it was as if
the town at the point in time when we studied it was a summation
of the archeology of American history." They continued, "In a word,
the culture of the town was stratified in terms of various periods of
American history as well as in its selective adaptation to contemporary institutions."[27] Something of this overlapping of historical
periods is evident in the LaPorte stories about the "Murder Farm,"
as well. The Diesslin and Nicholson family stories capture the
pioneer ethic, Gene McDonald's American Victorianism, and Martin Barlag's the Progressive Era. Yet these folk traditions are more
than inert survivals of bygone times; they are tangible effects of
conflicting value systems very much alive.

PART II

Gender, Kinship,
and Marriage Reversals

† 3 †

STRONG MAN OR STRONG WOMAN?

ON HIS DEATHBED in the Northern Indiana State Prison in 1909, Ray Lamphere told prison trusty Harry Myers that Belle Gunness was still alive, waiting for him in Chicago, disguised as a man. Long before his dying statement and long after, recurrent debates surfaced in LaPorte about the murderess's sexuality. As Louis Blake put it, "Fact, there's a lot of people doubted whether she was female or male."[1]

In June of 1908, the criminal anthropologist Cesare Lombroso, best known for his anthropometric evaluation of "born criminals," talked about women offenders in general and Belle Gunness in particular. His description, picked up in Chicago detective Clifton Wooldridge's discussion of the Gunness case, highlighted the blurring of acceptable gender lines. Lombroso said that "in general the moral physiognomy of the born female criminal approximates strongly to that of the male." He enumerated her masculine features: "The female criminal is exceedingly weak in maternal feeling, inclined to dissipation, astute and audacious, and dominates weaker beings sometimes by suggestion, and at other times by muscular force; while her love of violent exercise, her vices and even her dress, increase her resemblance to the stronger sex."[2]

Although Lombroso's list of those "virile characteristics" which produced the Gunness Monster is much more a cultural value judgment about men's and women's social roles than the scientific fact it was meant to be, it corresponds to sets of narratives told in LaPorte by older townspeople and country folk. Their stories deal with Belle's ambiguous sex by discussing her behavior in childbirth, her physical strength, and her masculine personal appearance and dress preference.

LYING-IN

Neighbor women's stories about the birth of Belle's youngest child, Philip, in the spring of 1903 set up a sexual uncertainty in the women's world of midwives and childbirth. Mrs. Swan Nicholson told her family that the door of the Gunness farmhouse was shut on her when she went up to help out at the time of delivery. Her son Albert remembered that Mrs. Gunness "looked like she might have a child any old day. Mother found out she should have been sick. Went up. [She] wouldn't let Mother in the house. After a while [she] produced a boy baby." Albert told Lillian de la Torre that his family interpreted Belle's asocial behavior as a sign that her delivery had been a sham.[3]

Their conclusions were shared by other neighbors, too. Dora Diesslin Rosenow remembered her mother's experience:

> And my mother went to call on her when this baby was supposed to have been born. And, when she got down there (it was just a day or so after), and she was out in the yard chasing pigs and running around! My mother says, "How can you do that, a new mother?" "Oh," she said, "the baby's in there in bed." She had him in a big bed, covered up, you know. (And, really, he was an adopted child. I think they were all adopted children.)[4]

Dora's gloss of the situation—"And, really, he was an adopted child. I think they were all adopted children"—extends Belle's nonmotherhood to Myrtle and Lucy Sorensen as well.

Frances Lapham Dawson, whose family's farm was also close to the Gunness place, told de la Torre a remarkably similar story about her mother's visit to Belle's farm house:

> Jennie came down, called Mother out of bed, "Mother has gotten a little baby boy."
>
> "How nice. I'll come over and help her in the morning."

She went over in the morning. So help me, she was by the cistern at the back door and she was washing the baby's clothes!

"You shouldn't be up!"

"Ah, in the old country they never go to bed after they get a baby!"[5]

None of the women, hardy farmwives themselves with many children apiece, or their son and daughters who related the stories to field researchers accepted Mrs. Gunness's response. Frances Dawson told de la Torre that her family felt that Belle had killed Philip's real mother and had taken her newborn son as a prop in a horrible masquerade. "Belle was as big as a man," Mrs. Dawson said, "maybe she was a man."

Another neighbor woman, a midwife, told Mary Swenson that she had been scheduled to go to help Mrs. Gunness at the time of Philip's birth. By the time that she was called, however, the baby had been born, bathed, and dressed—and looked too old to be a newborn. The midwife said that this incident gave her "further thought" that Belle was "way too masculine to be a woman." Although Mrs. Swenson was careful to say that this reading of the event was just one woman's opinion and not her own, she did say that many people had talked about the possibility of Belle's being a man in disguise.[6]

Was she? This cycle of narratives gives a multileveled response. Certainly, Belle did not *act* like a woman. She closed the door on a neighboring farm wife and called a midwife too late to assist at the birth, and so reversed the rural code of welcoming female help at childbirth. John Mack Faragher has reconstructed the "specifically feminine culture" in the nineteenth-century Midwest from his analysis of women's diaries, letters, and folkloric material. He finds that the separate worlds of men and women were particularly well defined in farm communities. Women depended on each other for information, "the things communicated within the kin family from mother to daughter, from sister to sister, or from 'granny' and midwife to young wife, neighbor to neighbor." They also depended on each other for companionship and socializing. Faragher writes, "It was from these common bases—the experience of being a woman, of childbirth and motherhood, of healer and nurse—that a specific female culture took form."[7]

Although male physicians were assisting at many home births

by the turn of the century, midwives were still delivering babies in country towns, rural areas, and urban ghettoes. Neighbor women still expected to assist the doctor in some way, to bring covered dishes for the new parents, and to help with the other children.[8]

Yet Belle's actions can be seen as metaphors of the shifts in medical practice that were undermining those feminine communal values. Barbara Ehrenreich and Deirdre English find that urban elite patterns of birth based on male physicians' care and maternity hospitals were spreading across the United States at just this time. Midwives were being outlawed in state after state; they were a class of health-care providers who were submerged in the male hierarchy of official medicine. Richard and Dorothy Wertz, in their *Lying-in: A History of Childbirth in America*, agree that the shift to male physicians was more clearly seen at the turn of the century, but that it was a culmination of a cultural preference, apparent even in the early colonies when laboring women chose male midwives to attend them, rather than a power play originating at the Johns Hopkins Medical School. Whichever the case may be, all authors agree that these years, as Wertz and Wertz put it, "began the major transformations in birth: from home to hospital, from suffering to painlessness, from patient care to disease care."[9]

Perhaps it is significant that LaPorte opened its first permanent hospital in 1900. Five sisters of the Order of the Poor Handmaidens of Jesus Christ opened Holy Family Hospital in a small frame house that was once a private home. Additions in 1914 and 1924 and its merger with Fairview Hospitals in 1966 to form the LaPorte Hospital attest to its success. Just as the new LaPorte Hospital opened in 1972, women around the United States were finding that safe hospital births left them alienated from family and friends.[10] Was Belle Gunness a man or simply a woman who had acquired (or feigned) urban tastes her neighbors could not yet comprehend?

And how does one explain her disclaimers of old-country strength? Did peasant women actually find birthing easier than their middle- and upper-class counterparts? An excerpt from Joanna Stratton's *Pioneer Women* suggests that such was not the case. Stratton writes that "childbirth itself was often the most difficult time of all." She then gives the case of the Kansas farm woman who delivered her own child, alone in the house with two other small children, while her husband was on a trip gathering winter firewood. Her daughter finishes the story: "My mother, having fainted a number of times in her attempt to dress the baby, had succeeded at last; and when my father came in he found a very uncomfortable but brave and thankful mother, thankful that he had returned home with the precious wood, and that she and the baby were alright."[11]

Yet Wertz and Wertz found that many people in the nineteenth and early twentieth centuries, physicians included, felt that lower-class women, especially Native American, black, and immigrant poor, suffered much less than others at delivery and made speedier recoveries. The "proverbial Indian squaw" who dropped her baby in between strides became a double-edged symbol, used somewhat differently by male and female authors. Male authors used the Indian woman as a symbol to show that painful births followed those women who left the domestic sphere that was natural to them and exhibited "unfeminine eagerness" and aggressiveness. Female authors, however, used the Indian woman as a symbol to show female self-sufficiency. She "not only did not need male attention in giving birth, *but she was like men in being strong and self-determined*" (pp. 109–128; emphasis added). The female narrators of the stories about Belle's chasing pigs and washing clothes at the cistern did not seem to take much stock in the Indian squaw as positive model, yet Belle herself may have used this myth of the natural woman and painless birth to her own advantage. The possibilities encoded in these stories remain, yet point to a second group of narratives, in which the murderess's muscular powers place her in the men's world of the field and the market.

THE STRONG-MAN MOTIF

Lillian de la Torre wrote that, in the aftermath of the Gunness fire, "tall tales were taking shape. The mighty Belle, the Hog Butcher of Indiana, was beginning to be Paul Bunyan's only rival. She could lift a calf, tote a trunk full of bodies, move a piano single-handed. People began to think they had seen her perform these feats" (p. 39). People certainly did talk about them, and most of these people were men. Clyde Sturgis told Stewart Holbrook that he had been a hack driver who found himself delivering trunks to the Gunness place late at night. He had tried to help Belle by cutting the rope tied around one particularly heavy trunk. She screamed at him to let the trunk be and then "picked it up off the porch like a box of marshmallows and lugged it inside" (pp. 130–31). The implication that a body or bodies were hidden in the trunk becomes submerged in Mrs. Gunness's Herculean feat.

John Nepsha, Jr. told me how his father learned from one of her ex-handymen that the murderess "was a real husky woman. Could pick up two hogs weighing over a hundred pounds under each arm [demonstrating by holding his arms out at both sides]. And this guy was a little shortie, you know!" Louis Blake said, "And then they tell this story about her going to auction sales, and maybe she'd buy a two-hundred-pound hog and would throw it up in her little cracky wagon that she had, that she drove with her horse. Load that pig all by herself. No one would ever help her." When I asked Gene McDonald if Belle was strong, he exclaimed, "Oh, wonderful. Why she could pick up two-bushel-and-a-half of wheat and just throw it in the wagon and never think nothing of it." Perhaps the tallest tale was told by *Indianapolis Star* reporter Harold Sabin when he wrote for Indiana's sesquicentennial that Belle had abnormal strength as a baby, could kill a hog with a knife at the age of ten, and could fight with her fists at the age of twelve.[12]

These tales, based on the reversal of the traditional strong-man motifs found in many folk literatures, have been sufficient proof for several tall-tale tellers and listeners that Belle Gunness was a man.[13] Again, the evaluation of this narrative cycle is difficult. Was Belle's superior strength real or imagined? LaPorteans generally agree that she did her own hog butchering, did much of her own farm work, and drove a delivery wagon—as well as dissected her murder victims herself. Faragher notes that hog butchering was one of the few areas where men's and women's farm work overlapped in the Midwest of the 1850s; usually, however, men from neighboring farms joined together for the slaughter of the animals, and the women prepared the bacon, sugar-cured the hams, rendered the lard, made the sausage, and used the cracklings. In unusual circumstances, a woman might help her husband slaughter and dress the animal itself (p. 52). The situation remained virtually unchanged through the 1920s in rural Indiana. A resident of north-central Indiana told Betty Miller: "I can remember us like butchering six to eight hogs at a time, and this again was a neighborhood get-together. There would be several farmers who would go together, and, say, they would butcher one week at one farmer's house and the next week at another farmer's house." And Harold L. Welkie, raised on a farm in Wanatah, Indiana, told Laurie Radke that all the neighbors came to help on butchering days. On the first day, the men selected the hog, shot it, bled it, scalded it, gutted it, and saved the head for head cheese. On the second day, the women took over. They carried the pork pieces into the kitchen and prepared hams, pork shoulders, bacon, and sausage. Often, young boys had the job of grinding sausage, as that was an arduous task as well.[14]

Belle, by butchering alone, reversed the communal pattern and subsumed both the male and the female roles. But did other women, as well? Would widows, especially farm widows who were strong, take up the tasks their husbands had left? Faragher suggests that Midwestern farm women themselves knew that the sexual division of labor was a code to which they would adhere, even though their diaries reveal that they actually helped their husbands in all sorts of tasks, such as driving a team, plowing, and bringing in the harvest (pp. 110–43). Was Belle Gunness a typical farm woman, or was she not? A series of questions—Was her strength magnified by tellers whose rules for gender were formed under more urbanized conditions? Was she a disguised man using the stereotype of the peasant woman once again to gain his own ends?—leads to a possible metaphorical reading of the strong-man narratives. In fusing men's and women's spheres in the agricultural domain, the Belle Gunness figure actually duplicated the transitional roles of women in the American work force under the urban influence at the turn of the century. At no time, before or since (perhaps with the exception of the 1940s, when married women entered war work in unprecedented numbers), did women leave rural communities and their ascribed place there and migrate to the cities for positions in the business world, formerly a male preserve.[15]

AMERICAN BEAUTY

Mabel Carpenter was a child of seven when she met Belle Gunness. The meeting highlights some of the distinctions between town ladies and farm women and moves the strong-man motif shared by men into the world of fashion shared by women. Mabel and her sister Leona had been stationed at the kitchen door of their aunt's house to tell Mrs. Gunness where to deliver produce.

> And my aunt tells my sister and I that this woman is bringing potatoes to the house and that we are to stay in the kitchen so that when she comes we can tell her. Well, in the meantime, I hear my mother and my aunt talking in the living room about this awful bad woman and that my aunt doesn't want to come in the [kitchen], she doesn't want to talk to her, she doesn't want to meet her.
>
> So, we're in the kitchen, Leona and I, my sister Leona and I, and my aunt and my mother were in the living room. So, all at once we see this wagon drive up, and I said, "Leona, here she comes" [in a whisper]. And this woman comes in a cracky wagon . . . . She had this one horse, and she was sitting on top of this seat. So, well all at once she lifts up this great big basket of potatoes and puts it on her shoulder, and I said to Leona, "Look," I said, "that lady put a big basket of potatoes on her shoulder" [still in a whisper]. And she marched right to the house.
>
> And, as I said, the nice, polite girls that we were, we simply opened the door for them, that was Mrs. Gunness. And we opened it up, and she set the potatoes down. And she says, "Where's your aunt?" And I said, "She wants them down in the basement." And I said, "I'll show you where she wants them." She says, "I know where they go. I know where the potatoes go." (So I'm going to go down in the basement to show her, this awful, bad lady!)
>
> So, she comes back up, and I'm standing there. And she says, "Where's your aunt?" And I said—well, she went to take a step forward—and I said, "My aunt isn't feeling well. She's got a bad headache." (Well, my aunt did suffer. She might even of had that headache.) So she said, "Well, your aunt owes me for," she says, "for potatoes this time and the time before."
>
> Well, I said, "My aunt said she would pay you for the potatoes the next time you come." "Well," she says, "I don't know about that." [The implication here is that Belle Gunness was aware that she would not be delivering potatoes again after her farmhouse fire.] And I thought, "Oh, my goodness."
>
> And that's when I looked her up and down. And that hat she wore with this plume or whatever was on the side! And then she had this great big jacket on, with this ripple around here [pointing to her upper arm], you know, leg-of-mutton sleeves and this enormous big skirt. And then I looked down and there was her shoes peeking out from underneath her skirt. And man's shoes. I thought, "Man's shoes. Now what's she doing with man's shoes on?"[16]

Lucia Egle would have answered that Belle wore men's shoes because she was a man. "I always said she was a man dressed up in a woman's clothing," she began, "because she'd, she would have a skirt that was one of these real *heavy* things, you know, that if you kicked at it, couldn't even dent it, you know! Such a stiff, black thing." Was a woman's body or a man's body concealed underneath? Mrs. Egle went on to catalog the rest of Mrs. Gunness's attire. "And then she wore a white blouse and had a collar up to here, you know" [gesturing to chin]. Did the high collar and shirred front cover a woman's bosom or a man's muscle? "And that knot of hair up there" [touching the crown of her head]. The severe bun perched atop Mrs. Gunness's broad face hardly seemed a woman's head of hair. "I can just still see her on [her] porch and I always said afterward, I said, 'You know,' I said, 'I believe she is more man than she is woman.'"[17]

Belle Gunness's strength and male-oriented occupations had already fused the separate worlds of men and women, and her clothes did the same. Yet the significance of her costume is as complex as the uncertain meanings of her isolation in delivery and her slaughtering of hogs. On the one hand, heavy farm work and produce delivery demanded appropriate work clothes, men's boots and jacket among them. Yet the plumed hat, rippled leg-of-mutton sleeves, and full blouse were vestiges of the most elegant urban styles of the Gay Nineties. And, on the other hand, Mrs. Gunness's comfortable mix of styles coincided with the advent of the tailored suits and sport clothes designed for the increasing number of women who were working outside the home.[18]

The people telling and listening to these three cycles of narratives were trying to work out some very practical problems. The stories helped them explain how Mrs. Gunness had the strength to kill men and dispose of their bodies once she had dismembered them. The stories helped people explain why Mrs. Gunness might have escaped her farmhouse fire. The charred, decapitated body found in the ruins seemed much smaller than Belle Gunness's as they knew her. And the stories helped confirm the theory that Belle had gotten away, for she could dress as a man again and have the perfect disguise for eluding the authorities.

Yet the symbolic uses of these narratives have also been compelling. The stories placed the murderess in between the cultural categories of male and female, as either a womanly-man or a manly-woman. Her confused and ambiguous gender was a microcosm for the conflicting class and regional gender roles available in the community at the turn of the century and an inversion of the ordered distinction once known. These stories symbolized both social change and the conflicts that accompanied these shifts. They also marked Belle Gunness as unnatural and placed her squarely in Lombroso's category of monster.

It is significant that this gender dialectic was not an issue for younger townspeople interviewed. The symbolic power of the above narratives is not relevant for groups who define order in ways other than the separation between men's and women's biology and social roles. When people in their teens and their twenties describe the murderess, what becomes an issue is her appearance and her ability to attract the men she later murdered, and not her essence as a woman. Most commented on her mannish appearance, as had the older residents, but with the implication that she was a lonely, unattractive woman rather than a man in woman's clothing. Debora Keller said, "Belle was a tremendously heavy woman with huge muscles and greasy hair; she resembled a man so huge and strong." Winnie Nillson described her as "a very large woman, and she was in the business of raising animals and slaughtering them for meat. She was very lonely, and so she sent her name to a foreign country where they have a column for lonely women who need men—something like a mail-order bride." Diane Mitzner simply said that Belle was "an unattractive woman who had come to settle in LaPorte."[19]

Younger residents have wondered how such an ugly woman could be so successful with the men she later murdered. Interviewer Barbara Howes recognized this contradiction when she wrote about her field research. She first presents one side: "One of the most common remarks stated was that of her appearance. Everyone seemed aware of what a large grotesque woman she was and that she had such uncommonly large hands." And then she presents the other: "It is also agreed that Belle had quite a way with men to be able to lure them from all over the country and then without the slightest remorse do away with them and her children." The contradiction was eliminated for at least one resident, Mendy Pugh, when she said that Belle Gunness "married many men and she was very nice-looking."[20]

This shift away from Mrs. Gunness's uncertain sex to her physical unattractiveness is a function of the present ideal image of a beautiful woman and the current democratized image of beauty which blurs class distinctions between urban elite and Midwestern farm styles, once more rigidly maintained. Lois Banner, in her social history of American beauty, shows the parallel development of the necessary beauty package each woman should possess and of the cosmetics industry in our consumer-oriented society.[21] All of Belle Gunness's physical characteristics—huge bone structure and billows of flesh—reverse the contemporary image of the American model, who has aquiline features and is extremely thin, boyish in shape but not manlike.

The tendency to contrast the mass murderess's physical shape to prevailing conceptions of beauty is nothing new. In earlier periods, however, if illustrations from popular literature are any indication, Belle's figure was actually shaped into the current fashion. The cover of the 1908 *The Mrs. Gunness Mystery* shows Belle Gunness as a Gibson girl leaning over a bedridden man about to give him poison. Pouring Mrs. Gunness into the hourglass figure of the image Charles Dana Gibson immortalized at the turn of the century shows the contemporary attempt to overshadow the voluptuous woman who was in style in the late Victorian period. (Belle Gunness looked much more like the uncorseted Lillian Russell, whose style was based ultimately on an immigrant model, than the aristocratic "New Woman.") Banner writes that the Gibson girl was "a symbol suited to an age exploring new modes of sensuality, but still infused with Victorian sentimentality and rectitude" (p. 166). She writes several pages later that her image was "symbolic of the hopeful changes of the age: the new movement of women into the work force, the new freedom of behavior between men and women, the new vogue of athletics promising healthier bodies" (p. 168). Belle Gunness as the Gibson girl shows the reverse side of these changes, the attendant tensions and fears of that uneasy transition from the Victorian age to the Progressive.

A British crime pamphlet of the 1920s shows Belle as a flapper, an even more difficult feat than the Gibson girl. She stands in a fringed party dress, one hand on hip, the other raising a wine glass, next to the title: "The Crimes of Belle Gunness: Murderess, Adultress, and Baby Farmer." (The latter two charges are not authenticated and will be discussed in the following chapter.) Banner finds the flapper image, too, richly symbolic of cultural changes affecting women's roles: "On the one hand, she indicated a new freedom in sensual expression by shortening her skirts and discarding her corsets. On the other hand, she bound her breasts, ideally had a small face and lips . . . , and expressed her sensuality not through eroticism, but through constant movement." (pp. 278–80). Banner finds her image one of "vivacity and fearlessness and a basic indifference to men" (p. 279). Gunness as flapper shows the negative flip side of the new sexual tensions.

Strangely enough, no pictorial image of Belle Gunness from the 1930s or 1940s exists. Her image might have merged imperceptibly with that of the film greats such as Greta Garbo, Joan Crawford, and Rosalind Russell, whom Banner finds to be the mature, professional, masculine models for women entering the work force in large numbers (pp. 280–83). It is the cover of Lillian de la Torre's 1955 *The Truth about Belle Gunness* which gives the next representation. Here, Belle is depicted as a Jane Russell type, dressed, or more properly undressed, in a filmy black lace negligee showing deep cleavage. The words "Men swarmed like flies to her embrace and one by one were loved—and died" complement the visuals. Banner's comment is appropriate here: "Fashions in clothing in the 1950s reflected the combination of social repression and sexual exploitation that characterized American attitudes towards women. More than anything else, fashions came to resemble those of the Victorian period" (p. 285). The illustration depicts the murderous power of a woman hidden in a bedroom and not accessible to public control. This tension underlying the concept of public order versus private disorder erupts in a cycle of narratives about Belle's fur coat.

THE FUR COAT

When Mrs. Howard McLane first came to LaPorte in 1918 as a young schoolteacher, she lived in Mrs. Ward's boardinghouse on First Street. Dinner-table conversations were always heated and often turned to the town's mass murderess. "They used to talk of what a large lady Belle Gunness was. She had immense hands and was always seen wearing an old fur coat." Dorothy Rowley, LaPorte County historian, remembered her grandparents' talking about Belle's coming to their farm auctions, wearing a sealskin cap and a man's fur coat, tramping around in the mud with the men, looking at the farm machinery while the rest of the women stayed up near the stove.[22]

At first glance, these brief descriptions sound just like those discussed earlier about Mrs. Gunness's sexually ambiguous dress and behavior. Yet they are more. When Mary Swenson recalled that Belle "had this big fur coat, and that was the one she had taken from her last victim,"[23] the coat becomes more than a sign of her masculinity; it becomes a sign of her depravity as well. Not only had she killed Andrew Helgelien, a South Dakota rancher whose body was the first dug up in her backyard on May 5, 1908, but she had the effrontery to walk around town in a garment distinctive enough to be recognized. She brought private chaos into the public realm.

On the day Andrew Helgelien's body was dug from her lot, the *Argus-Bulletin* reported that Belle had been seen wearing the coat on several occasions and "when asked concerning its purchase stated that it had been given to her by an admirer." Early in their courtship by mail, when Andrew was still debating whether to leave his ranch, Belle had urged him to come before the winter set in. She wrote in her October 29, 1906 letter, "Clothe yourself well on the way, put on a heavy fur coat and good warm shoes and everything." On November 22 of the same year, she wrote again, "Be sure and put good warm woolen clothes on and your big fur coat, so you will not catch cold on the way." When Andrew Helgelien finally arrived in LaPorte over a year later, in January of 1908, he was wearing the coat that Belle later wore.

The quotation from the November 1906 letter above has also been translated to read: "Procure some good new woolen underclothing, and a good big *bear*-skin coat, so you will not take cold on the trip" [emphasis added]. Eldora Burns, who remembered seeing the rancher at the Gunness farm, thought that his coat was "a big fur, brown, medium, shaggy, not buffalo." Bob and Ruth Coffeen had much the same memory:

> Bob: She even put the coat on to go downtown, to go to the bank. And stuff like that. The coat of one of her victims. Andrew Helgelien. Big heavy fur coat.
> Janet: And that was the style, too, wasn't it? Or was it some years later that beaver—men wore beaver coats?

Ruth: But I think this was different.
 Bob: Coarser.
Ruth: Uh-huh. More like *bear*.[24]

Since these stories about the fur coat are those shared most often by both men and women of all ages and at all times since the day of the Gunness fire in LaPorte, their popularity points to an enduring cultural message symbolically embedded in the fact that the murderess wore wild-animal skins. Gene McDonald's description of the coat's reversibility might guide us in the right direction for understanding the significance of these folk narratives. He told me, "And she used to wear a leather coat. I mean a cowhide coat. And when it rained, she wore it with the inside out, then the leather was on the outside; other than that, she wore it with the hair on the outside."[25] Belle's wearing the reversible coat corresponds to the imaginative reconstruction of one of her murders in *The Mrs. Gunness Mystery*: "Midnight came. And with the final stroke of the hall clock, there arose from the peaceful bed of Mrs. Jekyll, the bloodthirsty monster, Mrs. Hyde" (p. 68). The coat seems a fair outward sign of her inward nature. The beast within is revealed without. The following equation points out the symbolic equivalences:

Belle's Coat		*Belle's Nature*
leather side out	=	Mrs. Jekyll (human)
hair or fur side out	=	Mrs. Hyde (wild animal)

Like that of the animal bridegroom in the international folktale, Belle's animal skins are removable, yet they signal her awful mediation between the human and the inhuman. She becomes a primordial metaphor connecting man and beast, and in this liminal state she highlights culture's vulnerability in the face of nature in its wildest state. The fur coat narratives place her as a symbolic wild animal with whom no social relations are possible or desirable and who, therefore, remains the archetypical stranger.[26]

Orrin Klapp's analysis of Americans' categorizations of strangers corresponds to the conclusions drawn above. He discusses one particular class of strangers who go so far beyond our cultural conceptions of civility that they seem "alien not only to the group but to the human species." We call these strangers monsters and label them "fiend," "devil," "witch," "vampire," "ogre," and "Bluebeard."

Belle Gunness, in her fur coat, is firmly in this category. She has been labeled all these names and more, as we will discover in the next chapter.[27]

Klapp has suggested that the kind of society that would tend to label strangers in these ways would be closed, with high internal unity but with a threat of invasion or of some kind of crisis to the social structure. As we have seen in preceding chapters, many people in LaPorte have felt the boundaries of their town threatened by outside forces, and have had to confront shifts in social structures that they have held most valuable. Belle Gunness, as a stranger and as an unruly woman, becomes an appropriate symbol for marking changes in the social institutions of marriage and kinship, which we will explore in the following chapter.[28]

† 4 †

THE LADY BLUEBEARD

THE PRESS AND BOOKS on crime have usually been credited with giving Belle Gunness the label "the Lady Bluebeard," or its variations "the Female Bluebeard" and "Madame Bluebeard." The first such use in print appeared in a May 15, 1908 *LaPorte Argus-Bulletin* article which referred to the murderess as "the Modern Bluebeard." The term has had wide oral circulation, as well, so that, by 1972, when Winnie Nillson was interviewed, she could say with some accuracy that Belle "is widely known as the Lady Bluebeard."[1]

This label, however, was only one of many metaphorical names applied to Mrs. Gunness at the turn of the century. Epithets which referred to her relations with her victims included: "unnatural mother," "siren," "the Merry Widow," and "the Black Widow." Others referred to her methods of murder: "arch-priestess of poisoning," "Borgia of the cornfields" (with variations "dashing cornfield Borgia," "modern Borgia," and "bucolic Borgia"), "Queen of the Abattoir," "Belle, the Butcher," and "Mistress of Murder Hill." Still others referred to mythological and folkloristic prototypes: "ogress," "monster," "fiend," "fiend incarnate," "female vampire," "vampiress," "ghoul," "sorceress," and "the mail-order Circe," as well as to the "Bluebeard" allusions.

Why was the one metaphorical epithet "Lady Bluebeard"

70

selected and maintained for seventy-five years to the exclusion of
the others? If metaphor can be seen as a compressed story or a
condensed myth, then the answer is related to a growing tendency
for the community storytellers to use the fairytale "Bluebeard" as
an implicit model for talking about the Gunness murders. The
deeper question *why* the Bluebeard tale has come to structure the
community's folk art is related to an observable shift in the complex imagery used in discussing the case since the turn of the century, which, in turn, is related to transitions in American conceptions of family relationships.

When I asked Maxine Ford why she thought Belle Gunness was
called the Lady Bluebeard, she answered, "I suppose because
Bluebeard had killed so many women and she had killed so many
men. I imagine they tied it in with the story of Bluebeard." The
Bluebeard fairytale has two distinct but related plots. Both variants have Bluebeard, the wealthy ogre, murder multiple wives
who are sisters from peasant families. The youngest sister becomes
the last wife, who discovers the mutilated remains of the others. In
the literary versions, known to most of us through editions of
Charles Perrault's *Contes* (1697), the wife outwits the husband by
cleverly bringing her brother to her aid. In the oral versions known
throughout most of northwestern Europe—versions that may have
originated in Norway, the birthplace of murderess and victims
alike—the wife subdues her husband and resuscitates her sisters
by putting their severed limbs together.[2]

THE FORBIDDEN CHAMBER

Since no one in LaPorte had ever been inside Belle Gunness's
house or had any idea in which rooms she had murdered, dismembered, and stored her victims for burial, the idea of a single
"chamber of horrors" developed around personal-experience stories
taken as circumstantial evidence. The May 11, 1908 *Argus-
Bulletin* reported an interview with a fourteen-year-old Polish girl
who had done housework for Mrs. Gunness while her father had
done yard work in the summers of 1906 and 1907. The reporter
wrote that "Anna Brogiski, although the housemaid for several
months, says she never was allowed inside the mysterious room, off
the parlor, which is believed to have been the murderess's slaugh-

ter house." The article quoted Anna, who said, "The Gunness children . . . were afraid of their mother and said they didn't dare go in the room. I was warned to keep out and I minded. I don't know whether the door was kept locked for I never dared try it." Anna's testimony places Bluebeard Hall, as it was called in *The Mrs. Gunness Mystery* (pp. 75–76), off the parlor. Most subsequent accounts suggest that it was located in the basement. Lucia Egle remembered being shooed away from the cellar when she and several friends walked out to the Gunness farm in the last days of April 1908. The girls had come to play with Belle's daughters, Myrtle and Lucy Sorensen, but were also hoping to be driven home in Belle's pretty little pony and cart. When they reached the Gunness place, Belle was there to greet them. "But she was standing on her porch and had all her curtains down, all around the house, see. And you couldn't see in anywhere."

When Myrtle and Lucy suggested playing a game of hide-and-go-seek, their mother went back into the house, and the children started playing around in the yard, "any place you could hide." When one of the children hid in a cellar window well, Mrs. Gunness came out immediately to tell them to keep away from the windows. "She says, 'Stay away from the windows.' So, anyway, Myrtle, she comes and tells us that. So we took that for granted, and we didn't play too much hide-and-go-seek, because I don't think we were too enthusiastic about having very much fun. All we were thinking about was the ride home in that pony and cart, see." Mrs. Egle later interpreted Belle's guarding the cellar as a sign of the existence of her private morgue.[3]

Mrs. Egle's recollection coincides with the story told by Carrie Garwood Davis, Myrtle and Lucy's teacher at the one-room Quaker school on the Deckers' property. The teacher, as quoted in a May 11, 1908 *Argus-Bulletin* article, said that the girls had come to school the Monday before the fire, crying that their mother had whipped them that morning. "'We were on the cellar stairs,' said Myrtle, between her sobs, 'when Mama grabbed us and whipped us awfully and we are now afraid of her.'" Mrs. Davis repeated this story for the rest of her life. In 1975, she interpreted Belle's beatings as signs of her general abuse of her children, as well as a warning not to venture too near her "charnel house."[4]

The "forbidden room" motif spread from the secret room in

Belle's house to all the enclosed areas on her property. George Heusi remembered a childhood incident of 1907 when he was visiting his Diesslin cousins, Mrs. Gunness's neighbors.

I was six years old at the time. Can't remember which Diesslin girls were along—Louise, Anne, my sister, and myself. I think that was all. We were digging for sassafras root right in back of [Mrs. Gunness's] house along the fence line of the pig pen. There was a stile over the fence that joined the properties—oh, four or five steps. And she came out with a ball bat and chased us over the stile. She hit my sister Katherine in the back. *Oh, she was mean.* We didn't know why she was chasing us until later. We found out later. Two bodies were buried along the fence, right out in the street where the railroad tracks [Pere Marquette Railroad] cut across McClung Road, right this side of Fish Trap Lake.[5]

George's story dramatized the general statement made in *The Mrs. Gunness Mystery* that Mrs. Gunness kept her burial ground "sacred" (p. 47). Certainly, Frank K. Coffeen's story did the same. Because he had done some masonry work for Mrs. Gunness, he was called as one of the witnesses at the coroner's inquest held over the body of the decapitated woman believed to be Belle Gunness. His May 12, 1908 deposition reads in part:

I went fishing with a friend of mine and stopped at Mrs. Gunness's to borrow a rope for an anchor-line. I came up and looked around in the neighborhood of the barn, and then went from the barn toward the house. Before I got to the back door, she came out of the back door and she seemed to be kind of startled or scared. I asked her about borrowing the rope and she did not recognize me at all. She asked, "Who are you?" After I had explained who I was, she remembered me. She let me take the rope.[6]

Forty-four years later, when Frank Coffeen repeated the story to Lillian de la Torre, he recounted the situation somewhat differently. He repeated that he had taken a boat to Fish Trap Lake but had forgotten a rope for his anchor. He had walked up the driveway between the cedars and the barn and had come around to the back of the house, where Mrs. Gunness met him.

"Who are you?"

"I'm the mason. I want to borrow a rope."

"You know where it is, in the barn. Go get it. And don't return. Hang it on the gate."

He had gone out of the yard, saying to himself, "There's something wrong around here."[7]

These repeated records of "the rope story" give textual evidence for the shift in the narrator's perception of his encounter with the murderess. Belle's depicted character moved from startled to menacing, and the narrator's comprehension moved from unsuspecting to suspecting foul play. His son Bob told me the story twenty-four years later:

> My Dad—times was slack, and he and a friend, George Angel, were fishing out there, but they didn't have an anchor rope. It was right, right off the Gunness property. And my Dad had done enough work for Belle, and he knew the property, the barn. "Oh," he said, "I'll go up. It's a short way up here. I'll go up to Belle's barn and get a piece of rope."
>
> Well, after he did, he started across the yard, and Belle came bounding to the door like she was catapulted. "Mr. Coffeen, what are you doing on my property?"
>
> "Mrs. Gunness, I, I—we don't have an anchor rope, and I know you have some rope in the barn."
>
> "Well, get the rope and get off my property."
>
> *What he was doing, of course, was walking across part of her private graveyard.*[8]

In the serial transmission of the rope story from father to son, Belle's depicted character moved from menacing to forbidding, and the narrator's comprehension (this time Bob's gloss on his father's understanding) moved from suspicion to confirmation of Mrs. Gunness's murders. The anchor-rope narratives from 1908 to 1976 are records of the patterning process which invests the burial ground with the taboo quality it has in common with the forbidden chamber.

MUTILATED HUSBANDS

According to the 1908 coroners' reports, the bodies found in the Gunness lot, both those identified and those unidentified, included at least ten men, two women, and numberless bone fragments. Contemporary sources attributed the murdering of men, women, and children to Belle. In fact, *The Mrs. Gunness Mystery* put the murders into a nineteenth-century evolutionary sequence. Belle

practiced first on babies, worked up to girls and women, and
reached the apex of her powers with the men who answered her
matrimonial ads (p. 137).

Although popular reports of Belle's baby farm in Chicago never
seemed to be seriously considered in LaPorte, people did argue
about her maternal instincts and attitudes towards children.[9] The
evidence is indeed mixed. For every account of her cruelty to her
daughters and to the neighbor children, there is a corresponding
account of her motherliness and warmth. Stewart Holbrook wrote,
"But of all the lore concerning Belle, the most typical is a tale that
she was 'always kind to children and dumb animals.' This sort of
thing is a hoary old favorite with Americans" (p. 241). A May 7,
1908 *Argus-Bulletin* editorial began the dialectical tradition in the
print media:

> But while Mrs. Gunness was plotting to take life she was bestowing
> upon her children all the love of a mother's heart. She dressed them
> handsomely. She provided them with ponies and carts. No juvenile
> ambition went unsatisfied. She sent them to Sunday School, seeking
> to develop in them the religious nature which she had once experi-
> enced in girlhood in Norway, where the bestiality of her nature lay
> dormant. It was because of her intense devotion to her children, little
> bundles of petticoats that knew but sunshine that people were loath
> to believe that this mother had become a fiend incarnate, that human
> life had no value in her sight, and all for the possession of money,
> which could but bring her anguish of conscience.

Frances Dawson agreed with the editor's opinion. She remembered that "Myrtle and Lucy were always giggling, they were of an
age. They were happy children. I don't think she was ever mean to
the children because Jennie loved her. It was always 'Mamma.'"
Frances said that Belle "liked dogs, liked cats, liked all kinds of
animals, worshipped horses. She wouldn't kill a chicken; my
brothers used to kill them for her." Eldora Burns remembered that
Mrs. Gunness always wanted her to sit in her lap when she drove
the children to school. "Mrs. Gunness tried to be good to us. She
give us tablets and pencils and things." And, when butchering time
came in the fall, "she acted like she was afraid of blood" and always asked someone else to do it.[10]

Other neighbors remember Belle's bringing food to neighbor
children who had been burned or were quarantined with chicken

pox. They recall that she celebrated Christmas holidays with festivities especially planned for the children, too. Belle's love letters to her last victim, Andrew Helgelien, are filled with affection for young, growing things. She wrote on November 29, 1906: "I hope we will all be well and then we will be alright. Up to date we have been very fortunate in this respect as we have lived here over five years and I have never had a doctor bill to pay for either me or my children. This is something to be thankful for." She had written earlier, on September 2 of the same year: "I would enjoy seeing all your beautiful horses, as I am much interested in horses and other creatures. Could you not bring with you a pretty young driving horse? It would give us so much pleasure."

Her affection for Andrew was expressed in the same motherly terms. In a November 12, 1906 note, she asks him to dress warmly so that he doesn't catch cold (that fur coat again). She promises to bake him good Norwegian dishes when he comes. "We will have some good Norwegian coffee, waffles, and I will always make you a nice 'cream pudding' and many other good things," A week and a half later, she wrote again that "it is a shame that you cannot have some of our codfish and cream pudding as in the spring it is too warm for such. But I guess I can make you a cream pudding anyway."

These accounts simply don't mesh with older residents' stories about the death of Peter Gunness's child from his first marriage soon after he married Belle in April of 1902. Frances Dawson told her mother's story:

> When she married Peter, he had a daughter, Swanhilde, and a baby eight months old. Swanhilde is living. We were up there the evening before the baby died. The baby was on a blanket in front of the stove in the living room, playing and happy. Next morning Mother saw the doctor go by, watched, he went up there. He came back, the undertaker with him. Mother threw her shawl over her head [and went over to the Gunness place]. Mrs. Gunness said the baby died, strangled. Dr. Martin said afterwards she probably put the washcloth over its face. No inquest.

Mrs. Joyce M. Cook compressed the above history to a single sentence: "Peter brought with him a baby which died suddenly— and so did Peter!" Ann Jones, in her *Women Who Kill*, could find no evidence for this story, although she did find legal documentation to show that Peter Gunness did have a child who died with his first wife in childbirth.[11]

Stories about the death of Belle's ward Jennie Olsen are some of the most poignant narratives told by older townspeople and some of the most baffling. Like the other foundlings Belle had supposedly acquired in an early-day Chicago "welfare system," as Gene McDonald put it, Jennie was given to Belle when she, too, was eight months old, by her father, Ole Anton Olsen, at the death of his wife in 1890, when Belle and her first husband were still living in Illinois. After Belle became a widow in 1900 and Ole remarried, they began a battle for the custody of Jennie. And Belle won. She took Jennie with her to LaPorte in 1901, allowing her to visit the Olsen family only once, shortly after her own marriage to Peter Gunness. Jennie's brother and sister testified at the inquest over her body that Jennie hadn't been happy with the Olsens and had missed the LaPorte farm. Jennie returned to Mrs. Gunness, and relations with the Olsens were severed.

Mrs. Gunness's neighbors talked about the late fall of 1906, when Jennie was sixteen and already had two suitors. Frances Dawson remembered that her family hadn't seen Jennie for a week or so. When she went up to the Gunness place to inquire if Jennie was ill, Belle told her, "Oh, I forgot to tell you, I put Jennie in a girl's school in Wisconsin." Albert Nicholson remembered that she "come down here and told the folks she had sent Jennie to college. After a while she come down here with a letter and read it to the folks, but without the envelope, told what a good time Jennie was having at college. She read it aloud, took it back home with her. Mother never saw Jennie's college clothes." Albert also remembered that one of his friends had been one of Jennie's sweethearts. The boy would go up to visit with the girl on Sundays when Belle released her from the heavy farm chores. His deposition at Jennie's inquest is the earliest account of her disappearance.

I last saw Jennie Olsen alive about ten days before Christmas, 1906. I went to see her at Mrs. Gunness's. She told me she was going to Los Angeles to college. I told her that if she did not see me at Bowell's Billiard Hall, across from the Courthouse, to be sure and write to me, and she said she would. I told her I'd be out the next Sunday. She said, "Do come."

The next Sunday I went out. It was snowing, blowing. I went over to Foster & De Garmo's and hired a cutter. When I got to Mrs. Gunness's, I rapped at the door and asked for Jennie. Mrs. Gunness had a kind of grin on her face and said, "Why, Jennie has gone to Los Angeles, California." I said, "Is that so? How funny. She said she was coming over to see me before she went." She said, "Yes, she went Wednesday."[12]

The day of the April 28, 1908 fire, the local papers reported the police's efforts to track Jennie down to tell her about the tragedy before she returned to the farm. The irony of it was that Jennie's body was the second unearthed on May 5 (Andrew Helgelien's was the first)—the day on which she would have been eighteen years old. From the state of the body, which was identified by its teeth and a skirt wrapped around the skeleton, coroner Charles Mack determined it had been in the ground approximately two years. College for Jennie had been a finishing school indeed. There was unanimous agreement at the time that Belle had killed the ward that she had fought so hard to keep because Jennie knew too much about her mother's matrimonial and murder system. There was absolutely no agreement whether or not she had killed her children Myrtle, Lucy, and Philip, as well, for that depended on the major dialectic whether she herself had perished in the fire.

The roles of good mother and of death mother are in precarious balance in these contradictory narratives. Some people, such as Maxine Ford, felt that Belle Gunness had "two sides to her obviously." Albert Nicholson said, for instance, that she truly wept when she talked about missing Jennie, the girl she had so recently murdered. Others felt that she knew how to manipulate the middle-class cult of motherhood to her advantage. The rides in the pony cart, the good food, and the Sunday school rides were carefully constructed charades, as were the love letters to Andrew and the letter from Jennie. Historian Ann Jones suggests that Belle Gunness was so successful in carrying out and concealing her murders because she, like other women who killed, was so successful at playing the role assigned to her (pp. 356–57, n. for p. 137).

Contemporary popular-literature accounts of Belle's abducting girls for the white-slave trade are not known in LaPorte and appear to be consciously elaborative.[13] Eb Hill, the black hack driver who drove visitors out to view the "Murder Farm," however, did tell a story about a young woman's encounter with Mrs. Gunness that has entered oral tradition in the community.

One version has been recorded in the 1908 *The Mrs. Gunness Mystery* and is based on contemporary newspaper reporters' interviews with Eb Hill or with law officers who had questioned the hack driver. The other version is Gene McDonald's, recorded in 1975 and 1976. Gene had talked with Eb about the Gunness case on several occasions before Hill's death. The sources agree that Eb had picked up a pretty, well-dressed young woman at the train station in LaPorte in mid-January 1908 and had brought her to the Gunness place late in the evening. He had waited to see if she wished to return to Chicago by a later train.

At this point, the narratives diverge. *The Mrs. Gunness Mystery* has Mrs. Gunness open the door and invite the girl in:

> It was maybe, one half an hour later that the cabman heard suppressed shrieks in the house. He leaped down from his seat and stood wondering, uncertain for a moment. Then the bolts flew back and the door burst open. In the flood of light he could see the girl and Mrs. Gunness struggling. The former was screaming for aid. With a final wrench she freed herself and sank in a faint. The widow slammed back the door, fastened the bolts and hastily put out every light.
>
> The driver carried the young woman to his carriage. She regained consciousness, but was hysterical. "Oh, it was terrible," she kept shrieking. "Oh, it was terrible. Take me away. Save me, oh, save me!" The girl continued in that condition until the depot was reached and was still hysterical when she boarded a train back to Chicago. [Pp. 44–54]

The girl had *either* "witnessed a murder or was herself attacked," but had managed to escape because Belle had not yet perfected her techniques of murder in this account.

Gene's version is much more specific:

> [The young woman] went to the front door, and she couldn't get in; then she went around to the back door, and she came out screaming. She wanted to get out of there as quick as she could. She said, "That woman had a man on the kitchen table, cutting him up!"[14]

For Gene, the girl, who had come to have an abortion, had only witnessed a murder and was only a potential victim at best. The man so murdered was Andrew Helgelien, believed to be killed by Belle on the evening of January 14 with the help of her handyman, Ray Lamphere.

Gene's story points to a shift in community perception of who Mrs. Gunness's victims were. At present, most people in LaPorte have heard of Andrew Helgelien, but hardly anyone remembers the nameless girl who struggled with Mrs. Gunness on the front steps or inadvertently saw Helgelien murdered when she went to the back kitchen door. Almost everyone remembers Peter Gunness, but his infant child's sudden death is as unremarked as its name. And even Jennie Olsen, once the subject of so many peoples' sympathy, is rarely discussed. Most people say, simply, that Belle was a woman who killed men, more specifically, a wife who killed husbands, although Mads Sorensen and Peter Gunness were the only two to whom she had been married. The others were would-be suitors whom Belle had introduced around town as her "cousins" or "brothers" and whom her children called "uncles."

Gene's story points to a second selective process. From coroners' reports and pathologists' examinations, there is evidence that Belle Gunness, like any good Victorian villain, had practiced overkill. She apparently drugged, bludgeoned, and then dismembered her victims with a meat cleaver. *The Mrs. Gunness Mystery* put it so well: "Some arsenic, a little chloral, a bottle of chloroform, a few keen-edged scalpels and dissecting knives, and Belle was prepared to enter into the wholesale murder business" (p. 45).

At the time that the multiple murders were discovered, people talked about all the methods, actually considering poisoning more often than the others. Joe Maxson, for example, testified at Ray Lamphere's trial in November 1908 that Belle had given him drugged fruit the evening before the fire. The reporter who reviewed that day of the trial in the *Argus-Bulletin* warned readers to beware of a "Gunness lemon" which was converted into a lethal variety by the Gunness system of murder. Joe's sister, Martha Alderfer, remembered his testimony many years later:

> They were in the dining room, playing wth the kids. She gave each an orange. Joe said he'd eat his later.
> "You'd better eat it, maybe you won't get another treat from me in a long time."
> He eats it, gets sleepy, goes up to bed, leaving them in the living room. He got upstairs [where he slept in a porch room in a wooden structure at the back of the brick house].
> After a while she come upstairs, opened his door, and looked in. He roused up, "What's the matter? Somebody sick?"
> "Just wanted to see if you're asleep."

[He got up and] locked the door. Thought if she wanted him, she could knock.[15]

Thanks to his hearty constitution, to his foresight in locking his door, and to his bedroom's location off the main house, Joe Maxson lived to smell the smoke the next morning and to tell the tale to coroner, judge, neighbors, relatives, and sideshow audiences in subsequent years.

Almetta Hay, who had walked out to view the Gunness farm herself as a young girl, said, "I don't know how many men she killed. She lured them, fed them, then poisoned them." Mrs. Hay's summary of Belle's deeds is expressed in a ballad, no longer extant, which suggests that Belle's knife-wielding propensities were seen as secondary to her powerful "mickey finns."

> Now, all these men were Norska folk
> Who came to Belle from Minn-e-sote;
> They liked their coffee, and their gin:
> They got it—plus a mickey finn.
> And now with cleaver poised so sure
> Belle neatly cut their jug-u-lur [sic];
> She put them in a bath of lime,
> And left them there for quite some time.[16]

Many older residents felt that Belle had dismembered her victims once she had poisoned them only to make their burial easier and less conspicuous.

By the time that Ruth Coffeen wrote her ballad on Belle Gunness in 1947, the emphasis had shifted to the bludgeoning/dismemberment mode of death for her unfortunate suitors. Remember the stanza quoted in chapter 1:

> Each suitor who came a courtin'
> Must first his bride endow
> And then that day without delay
> He fell for her—and how.

And the first chorus lines:

> Lay that cleaver down,
> Lay that cleaver down.
> Cleaver-cloutin' Mama
> Lay that cleaver down.

Lines from Dallas Turner's 1976 ballad "Belle Gunness" are similar:

> So big, mean and ugly, she stayed to herself.
> A sharp cleaver lay on her slaughter-pen shelf.
>
> . . .
>
> Men came to Belle Gunness to share food and bed
> Not knowin' that soon they'd be knocked in the head.[17]

Nineteen-year-old Debora Keller's statement about Belle's
methods is typical for her age group: "And do you know how she
killed her victims? She bashed them in the head with an axe. And
then she chopped up their bodies and buried them in gunny sacks
in her yard." Bob Fischer condensed Belle's techniques into a
single action when he said, "She took an axe and chopped up their
bodies while they were sleeping." This change of perception con-
forms to the Bluebeard pattern of murder by dismemberment.[18]

A third selective process has occurred regarding the nature of
Belle's private graveyard on her property. Although it was sus-
pected that bodies were strewn all over the yard when they were
first discovered, most of the bodies found had been buried in
garbage-filled pits within an enclosed area about 150 feet behind
Belle's house, southwest of the apple orchard and the marshy
ground of Lower Fish Trap Lake. Belle Gunness had both pigpens
and kitchen and truck gardens in this area. At the turn of the century, most legal and popular sources concentrated on Mrs. Gunness's death garden. Coroner Charles Mack's report on the inquest
of one of the victims concluded: "At the east end [of the grave] were
two or three rows of boulders under the wire fence which ran between the garden, in which this grave was, and the runway on
hillside toward the marsh on the east." A witness at Andrew
Helgelien's inquest said that the hired man Joe Maxson had filled
up a hole dug for compost "in the garden" in March 1908 which had
contained Helgelien's body for just over two months.[19]

The Mrs. Gunness Mystery waxed eloquent on the private and
paradoxical nature of this garden:

> As to the disposal of victims—what better than a garden? So Bella
> built her death garden. Adjoining the house it was. As the widow
> crooned her foster babes to sleep of a summer evening or chanced to

stand at the window and gaze out through the apple trees, the little private murder cemetery would always be before her eyes, always where she could keep strict vigil over the bones she planted there. [p. 46]

By the 1940s, the community focused on the hog lot or pigpen and not on the garden. Glen Ott's description is representative of the community's present perception of the Gunness burial ground: "Them bodies up there in that hogpen, you know, wasn't too deep. Now in the hogpen there, I would say, um, probably four or five foot deep. Well, that there, the pigs rooting around, you know, wouldn't leave no sign of a grave or anything." The movement from garden to hog lot is consistent with the Bluebeard pattern of dismembered wives hanging from meat hooks in the secret chamber like so many sides of beef. Belle is now the Butcher of Indiana.[20]

Gene McDonald's version of "The Girl in the Cab and Her Seance with Death" (p. 79) is a transitional text in its use of imagery. Within Gene's story, Belle Gunness's kitchen table is in a mediating position. It is the point in space where LaPorte storytellers have located the murderess feeding, poisoning, aborting, and dismembering her victims. It has qualities in common with both the "death garden" and the "hog lot." The following diagram outlines the table's vegetable and animal associations:

KITCHEN TABLE

Vegetable Associations (Female)	*Animal Associations (Male)*
victims: babies, girls, women	men (husbands)
methods: poison in coffee and fruit	bludgeoning by axe or dismemberment by meat cleaver
burial sites: death garden	hog lot

abortion

In Gene's story, Belle replaces the girl's scheduled abortion with Andrew Helgelien's dismemberment on her kitchen table, which literally turns towards the animal imagery which typifies most recent discussion. The earlier vegetable imagery correlates with Belle Gunness's maternal image. In contrast, the later animal imagery is associated with the Belle Gunness who is a wife, albeit a deadly one.

On one level, the shift in imagery corresponds to a shift in general cultural perceptions of murder. In her *Women Who Kill*, Ann Jones remarks that "alleged poisoning became the crime of the [nineteenth] century" (p. 102) and that "the poisoning wife became the specter of the century—the witch who lurked in woman's sphere and haunted the minds of men" (p. 77). The cases in Hartman's *Victorian Murderesses* support this generalization. The twentieth-century conception, perhaps molded by the carnage of two world wars, gangland-style killings, and urban crime, is oriented towards the "blood and guts" slaughter technique. Witness the oral circulation of modern belief tales of axe murders and the mass production of "splatter" horror films, in which chain-saw murders figure prominently.[21]

On another level, however, the shift from Belle's maternal to wifely presence correlates with a shift in marital concerns. Elaine Tyler May, in her *Great Expectations: Marriage and Divorce in Post-Victorian America*, analyzes divorce cases between 1880 and 1920 to understand why the percentage of broken marriages skyrocketed after the turn of the century. She notes that the earlier cases were built on either spouse's violation of marriage roles that were commonly accepted. Discussion of whether Mrs. Gunness was a good or a bad mother fits this Victorian concern with a woman's properly filling a role designated for her within the domestic sphere. May finds, however, that later divorces were based on either spouse's disappointment in personal and monetary fulfillments they learned to expect in a marriage. Women divorced their husbands because they did not satisfy them in either of these ways.[22]

Hartman and Jones find that some women killed their husbands for much the same reasons that others had divorced them. In earlier periods, wives had killed to remove themselves from marital arrangements in which they had had little personal say. Later murderesses had killed their spouses because of shattered expectations in marriages they themselves had freely chosen. May suggests that the romantic expectations for a marriage companionship, built on the base of late capitalism, more leisure time, and women's entering the work force, could not be met in many marriages, and so they foundered.[23] The cultural disjunction between romantic ideal and marital reality that Americans face in the twentieth century seems to be the major concern embedded in the stories about Belle's loving, then killing, multiple husbands. The connections between her mass murders and the rising divorce rate are tangibly expressed in two LaPorte residents' comments about serial monogamy!

Dora Diesslin Rosenow told me this little story about her family's unorthodox neighbor:

> My aunt used to come out on a Sunday, and mother and her were sitting outside, and they saw Mrs. Gunness walking back in her orchard with one of these fellows she had there, and my aunt said, "What is she—I wonder what she does with them?" And my mom said, "Maybe she kills them! Who knows?" And then she had a bedroom where they would sleep towards our house, and, after this all took place, she'd air out that bedroom and clean. The curtains would be flying out, and my mother would say, "Well, she got rid of *another* one!"[24]

Henry Johnson, whose family had farmed in the area for several generations, summed up Belle's operations: "She advertised her place at $8,ooo. And you had to have the same amount to come and get married to her. Being a complete partner, see? Ya, they'd come there. A couple of days, they disappeared. She got their $8,ooo, and they'd get a hunk in the head [laughing]! Then she'd advertise for *another* man."[25]

Belle as the Lady Bluebeard reverses the patriarchal position of the ogre husband in the folktale. Given ethnographic evidence about marriage as the institutional subordination of women by men, if not cross-culturally, at least consistently for much of western societies' histories, then the ogre and his mutilated wives are fantastic and distorted enlargements of real situations. By reversing the sexes of this fairytale pattern, stories about Belle Gunness, although equally grotesque, also invert the gender relationships and the power structures traditionally operating in the Victorian conception of marriage. The Gunness stories highlight that norm by inverting it through the figure of an abnormal but powerful woman on top. They also are vehicles for looking at the sweeping social changes affecting that norm. They trace the change, if not to wifely dominance then to one of a changed equality. The figure of their local mass murderess has conveniently given LaPorte townspeople a ground in which to test these changes, some to condemn them, others to see them as possibilities, most to sense the new sets of cultural tensions accompanying social transmutations.[26]

THE BROTHER AS HERO

One of the most enduring and widespread cycles of narratives in LaPorte is the story of Asle Helgelien's searching for and finding the mutilated remains of his brother Andrew on the Gunness grounds on May 5, 1908. Asle, as a witnes at Andrew's inquest on the same day, gave a testimony which pivoted around the axe murder of his brother on Belle's kitchen table the night of January 14. He reported that he and his brother had worked neighboring ranches in South Dakota for fifteen years after emigrating from Norway. When Andrew left for a week's visit to Indiana on January 2, 1908 and hadn't been heard from for almost two weeks, Asle began to worry about him. By March, he was terribly concerned, because he "had heard there was a rich widow here in Indiana advertising in a Norwegian paper for a Norwegian husband (the hired men on my place and on my brother's place joked one another about this)." He had also discovered Andrew's two-year correspondence with Belle and his withdrawal of savings for a mortgage on Belle's farm.

Asle began making inquiries, even hiring a detective to check into the situation in LaPorte. The LaPorte post office, police station, and bank verified Belle's existence and Andrew's short visit in January. When Asle wrote to Belle herself in April, she responded that Andrew had indeed come to her farm but had since "gone to Norway." When notice of the April 28th fire reached him in South Dakota on May 1 (a bank clerk in LaPorte had sent him a newspaper clipping), Asle took the next train east and arrived in LaPorte on May 3.

Spending the nights with the Nicholsons, Asle began his own investigations of the Gunness property. On May 5, he decided to dig in the soft spots in the yard that hired man Joe Maxson and neighbor D. M. Hutson had recently filled in with rubbish. His deposition is a powerful personal account of what happened next:

> After we had been digging a little, I noticed an awful bad smell. Mr. Maxson told me Mrs. Gunness had put a lot of tomato cans and fish cans there. Maybe it was they made it stink. We struck something hard and covered with a gunny sack. Then we saw the neck of a body and an arm.
>
> I believe that the body in question, the first one unearthed in the garden in the Gunness place, is that of my brother, Andrew K.

Helgelien. I do not *believe* it, I am *sure* of it. . . . When you have been
with your brother every day for fifteen years, you know him.[27]

He repeated his dramatic narrative again as a witness for the
state in Ray Lamphere's trial on November 16, 1908. His statement was a key text within the courtroom context. It changed the
nature of the audience, for women returned in great numbers to
hear his story, despite initial barring and a clergyman's denounc-
ing their presence. And it changed the nature of the trial verdict.
Designed to present state's evidence against the defendant by implicating him in Andrew's death, it actually proved a better case
for the defense by showing the murderess to be a woman capable of
inhuman deception. Belle's eighty love letters to Andrew placed
next to his dissected body convinced jurors that she just might have
duped the defendant by setting him up as the prime suspect in her
murder. And that was the defense's position.

Asle, in describing Belle's artful letter writing, which both con-
formed to and subverted the literary conventions of courtship, told
his courtroom audience how clever Belle Gunness was, how she
was able to use terms of endearment and Norwegian references to
draw his lonely brother to her. He said, "I did not know these
things until long after, when the letters came into my possession
and the *ogress* began writing to me" [emphasis added]. His reference to the fairytale monster pulled Belle Gunness, the real woman, closer to the fantastic Bluebeard: brother is pitted against ogress wife much as sister is pitted against ogre husband in the
tale.[28]

The moment of discovery, of brother finding brother, has been
selected for retelling in LaPorte for seventy-five years. Although
the names of the two brothers are not always known, their relationship is always stated. An analysis of three sample narratives
will show the contrasts developed between the brother's faithful
search and the ogress's brutalities. *The Mrs. Gunness Mystery*, in a
chapter labeled "The Detective," developed the contrast by comparing Asle's "simple" character to Belle's "designing" one:

It took him a long time to reason out, as he sat puffing his pipe at
sunset on his far western ranch that Andrew might have fallen into
the clutches of a designing woman and been fleeced. His mind did not
work by impulse. And it took even longer time for his simple brain to

develop a suspicion that Andrew might have been slain for his purse of gold.

Once Asle came to this conclusion, however, he pursued it to the end. "This quiet Norwegian quietly pressed his search for the missing brother until with his spade he uncovered in the private burying ground of the Widow Gunness the bones of the brother whom he sought" (p. 108).

Henry Johnson, eighty-nine at the time of our interview, learned much about the Gunness case from a brother who had once hired out as a drayman for Belle. As a milkman, he had stopped at farms and at customers' homes along his route and developed audiences and contexts for his verbal art. His wife and their eight children formed a more intimate audience for his tale telling. In his story, Asle and Belle are equally perceptive. The victim Andrew is the one who is simple-minded:

> She advertised her place at $8,000. And you had to have the same amount to come and get married to her. Being a complete partner, see? Ya, they'd come there. A couple of days, they disappeared. She got their $8,000, and they got a hunk in the head [laughing]. Then she'd advertise for *another* man. She was getting quite a multitude even then.
>
> So another fellow was going to answer her, and his brother said to him, "You'd better not." Says, "I realize what this place is." Said, "You won't live more'n two or three days."
>
> "Aw," [Andrew] says, "you're crazy." So he went.
>
> [Asle] says, "When you get there, I want you to write to me at once, at least once a week. And when you quit writing, I'll come and dig you up." So he just wrote him one letter and he quit.
>
> Well, [Asle] comes there right away and asked the boys [Joe Maxson and D. M. Hutson], "Have you got a shovel?"
>
> "Ya."
>
> Said, "Any digging going on here lately?"
>
> "Oh, yes, they buried a pile of junk right out there."
>
> Says, "Which was the last—where was the last hole dug?" [Joe] told him. He's digging for her, see. And covered 'em up. [Asle] just dug his own brother right up![29]

The contrasts that Henry developed in the play of dialogue, Maxine Ford developed in explanatory interpolations or glosses on her narrative. Maxine, who has learned about the Gunness case through a network of oral and literary sources, has Asle outwit the ogress Gunness by revealing her murders to the world. There is, in fact, an oral tradition in LaPorte that Belle Gunness set fire to her farmhouse when she guessed that Asle Helgelien would pursue the search for his brother:

> But she always specified in her letters to these men—after she advertised in the lovelorn magazines, she would specify: "Don't tell your family where you are going. Bring all your money. Sell all your property. But keep it a secret. Don't tell anyone where you're going." *Well, then you didn't have a social security number, and you didn't write or send telegrams. And you didn't call people up like you do now.* And so these men would come here.
> *She really liked it better if you had no family at all. Then she was safe.* But, you see, that's the one slip-up. Andrew Helgelien had a brother, Asa, I believe. But he came to LaPorte. And he found a soft spot as he walked over the farm. And he was suspicious. I think he dug himself. I think he dug up, strangely enough, the body of his brother.[30]

Because the fantastic world of the folktale could not be wholly translated to the historical world of community event, the brother as hero could not conquer, the ogress could not be conquered, and the sought-for person could not be saved. Asle Helgelien could not put Andrew's severed body together again and magically resuscitate him as did the heroine in "Bluebeard." Yet he symbolically did just that when he had Andrew reburied in Patton cemetery in LaPorte, under a marble tombstone whose epitaph marks the brother's fight against the wife:

ANDREW K. HELGELIEN
1859–1908

———

The Last Victim of the
Gunness Horror
Remains Found by His Brother
Asle K. Helgelien
May 5, 1908

The folktale triangle ogre husband-sisters-wife fantastically projects real stresses in the kinship system between "blood" and "in law" relationships. The gender reversals in the Gunness stories (ogress wife-brothers-husband) still pit spouse against siblings, but in the familar setting of an American small town. Data for American kinship patterns indicate, furthermore, that the split between biologically related relatives and those connected by marriage is weighted. For most Midwestern, middle-class, white Americans, consanguineal kin have "real" ties, while affinal kin do not.[31] Maxine Ford's statement that Belle Gunness "really liked it better if [prospective marriage partners and murder victims] had no family at all" shows, through reversal, that the proverb "Blood is thicker than water" is still considered the best strategy for dealing with kinship conflicts in American family life.

This weighting in favor of blood relatives, once congruent with the extended kinship system which historian Richard Jensen finds to be the norm in the preindustrial Midwest, is in direct odds with the rise of the nuclear-family structure we recognize as part of modern society.[32] Andrew Helgelien's gravestone is a visible reminder of this cultural conflict. The words carved on its marble face form an abstract script of the stories presented above. The community is reminded of a social paradox: marriage as a bond between a man and a woman unites them, yet splinters their families of origin. The figure of Belle Gunness, standing with an axe over a fallen suitor, is an apt symbol for the spouse as stranger. And the figure of Asle Helgelien, as the brother searching, is an apt symbol for the extended kin group. Together, they point to the slippage between cultural values in marriage.[33]

Innbygde, Selbu, in the province of Trondheim, Norway, where Belle
Gunness was born in 1859. Photograph courtesy of Dr. Kjell
Haarstad.

Belle Gunness as the bride of
Max Sorensen, Chicago,
Illinois, 1884. Photograph
courtesy of the LaPorte County
Historical Society Museum.

92

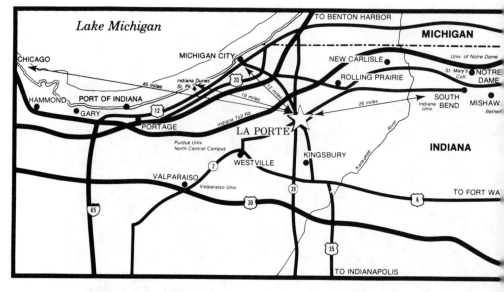

Current map of LaPorte,
Indiana, from a 1974 Chamber
of Commerce publication.

Line drawing of Belle as a baby
guillotining her dolls, from the
1908 *The Mrs. Gunness
Mystery*. Courtesy of the
LaPorte County Historical
Society Museum.

Artist's depiction of Gunness farmhouse and property before the
April 28, 1908 fire. Location of buried bodies noted. Reproduced by
courtesy of the LaPorte County Historical Society Museum.

Belle Gunness and her
children, Lucy and Myrtle
Sorensen and Philip Gunness,
1904. Photograph taken by
Henry Koch, LaPorte, Indiana,
courtesy of the LaPorte County
Historical Society Museum.

Belle as Gibson girl on cover of *The Mrs. Gunness Mystery,* 1908. Photograph by Kevin Swank, courtesy of the LaPorte County Historical Society Museum.

Belle as flapper on cover of British crime pamphlet, n.d. but ca. 1920. Reproduced by courtesy of Lillian de la Torre.

Belle as Jane Russell type on the cover of the 1955 *The Truth about Belle Gunness*. Photograph by Kevin Swank, courtesy of the LaPorte County Historical Society Museum.

Papier-maché cast of Belle Gunness, at the LaPorte County Historical Society Museum's Gunness exhibit. Photograph by Andrea di Tommaso, courtesy of the LaPorte County Historical Society Museum.

Jennie Olsen, Belle's ward.
Photograph courtesy of the
LaPorte County Historical
Society Museum.

Joe Maxson, the handyman
who discovered the fire, before
his employment with Mrs.
Gunness. Photograph courtesy
of Lillian de la Torre.

Gunness victims' bones in Gunness shed converted to temporary morgue, 1908. Photograph courtesy of the LaPorte County Historical Society Museum.

Andrew Helgelien, the last of Belle Gunness's victims. Photograph courtesy of the LaPorte County Historical Society Museum.

Asle Helgelien, who discovered his brother's body on the Gunness farm. Photograph courtesy of the LaPorte County Historical Society Museum.

Gunness farm after the fire. Photograph courtesy of the LaPorte County Historical Society Museum.

Finding bodies in the Gunness farmhouse basement after the fire.
Photograph courtesy of the LaPorte County Historical Society
Museum.

Ex-gold miner Louis Schultz panning for Belle Gunness's teeth in
the ashes of farmhouse. Photograph courtesy of the LaPorte County
Historical Society Museum.

$4,OOO.OO
REWARD
for the Capture Alive
of
Belle Gunness
The Sorceress of
MURDER FARM
who
SLEW 35 PERSONS

Read This Book!

Back cover of *The Mrs. Gunness Mystery*, 1908. Photograph by Kevin Swank, courtesy of the LaPorte County Historical Society Museum.

Ray Lamphere. Photograph courtesy of the LaPorte County Historical Society Museum.

Defense attorney Wirt Worden and defendant Ray Lamphere. Photograph courtesy of the LaPorte County Historical Society Museum.

Jurors for Lamphere trial. Photograph courtesy of the LaPorte County Historical Society Museum.

April 29, 1931 *LaPorte Herald-Argus* front-page photograph comparing 1904 photograph of Belle Gunness with a 1931 one of Esther Carlson. Reproduced by courtesy of the *LaPorte Herald-Argus*.

Author Lillian de la Torre as Belle Gunness in the one-act play *The Coffee Cup*, 1952. Photograph courtesy of Lillian de la Torre.

PART III

Economic and
Political Upheaval

† 5 †

COINING CUPID'S
WILES

WHEN ANN JONES CALLED Belle Gunness a "Bluebeard with a profit motive" (p. 127), she touched the web connecting marriage and economics that underlies all the folk art about the mass murderess. Most authors who have written about Belle and most townspeople who have talked about her agree that she killed her suitors for gain. Olive W. Burt classified the case under the heading "The Profit Motive" in her *American Murder Ballads and Their Stories* (pp. 72–76). Quotations given throughout the preceding chapters support LaPorte resident Mary Swenson's contention that murder was Belle's way "to bolster her own bank account."

No one agrees on just how much money the Lady Bluebeard acquired through insurance claims, mortgage payments, and outright deposits made by her unwary suitors. The LaPorte bank which carried her account reported a $700 balance at the time of the fire, but this amount is considered a pittance by those who believe that she stashed much more in various hiding places. Estimates range from $2,000 to $90,000 and are part of a tradition of hidden treasure in the vicinity of her property. Whatever the amount, Bob Coffeen has said that his father, Frank, had always been "paid cash on the barrel head so to speak" when he had done Belle's masonry work. Nowhere are the marriage-and-money connections more apparent than in a cycle of stories about the murderess's making sausage from her victims, a logical extension of the animal associations with men, developed in the last chapter.

SWEET SAUSAGE

Belle's treatment of her husband/victim Peter Gunness is usually associated with sausage making by people in LaPorte today. Peter died on December 16, 1902 in the hog-butchering season. On the day of his death, he had helped his wife make sausage. Belle said in her deposition at the inquest held two days later that "he was in town and got things to make sausage in and helped me along as best he could. After I put the children to bed, he ground some meat for me." The sausage making indicates husband and wife were working as a team, both as a couple and as an economic unit, the norm for a preindustrial Midwestern family.

Peter then sat in the parlor, reading and writing, while Belle stayed in the kitchen, stuffing the casings and washing out the sausage grinder, which she set on the back shelf of the stove to dry with a crockery bowl of brine for head cheese. What happened next is not known, although Peter was found lying face down in the parlor with his nose broken and a hole in the back of his head in the early hours of the next morning. The bowl of brine and the sausage grinder were on the floor in the kitchen.

Belle told the coroner that her husband had gone to the kitchen to get his shoes, which were warming near the stove, and to lock up before they went to bed. She was in the parlor, heard a loud noise, rushed into the kitchen, and found him holding his head in his hands. "'Oh, Mamma,' he says, 'I burned me so terrible.'" She had thought he had accidentally knocked the brine off the stove and burned himself. She rubbed him with vaseline and liniment, then went to bed with their daughters after fixing a place for him on the lounge in the parlor. Several hours later, he woke her up:

> He was over by the door and calling, "Mamma" so fast as he could and so the children waked up and I was trying to think and said they should keep quiet, that I had to go to Papa, that Papa was burned. I tried to put my clothes on because it was so cold. I went down the steps and when I came down he was walking around the room and saying, "O Mamma, Mamma, my head." I asked what the matter was. "My head, my head," he says, "it is like something going on in my

head." "Papa," I said, "What are you talking about?" I said. "Let me see what it is, I supposed you have rubbed off the skin."

"Oh, my head, my head."

"Well, if you think it is best I had better send for the doctor," I said, and I went upstairs and got the girl [Jennie] up and she went over to Nicholson's and when I came down from upstairs I found him on the floor and he was holding his head, and said, "O, Mamma, I guess I am going to die."

Jennie roused the Nicholsons by beating on their door with a poker. Swan and his son Albert came over right away, Mrs. Nicholson somewhat later. Swan sent Albert to town, and he returned with the coroner, Dr. Bo Bowell, who pronounced Peter Gunness dead.

The inquest was held at the Gunness home two days later, because the postmortem report that Gunness had died from brain hemorrhaging due to a blow on the head did not tally with Belle's account of her husband's burning. Only when questioned directly by the coroner at the inquest did she mention that she didn't know how his head got hurt: "I don't know doctor, I picked up the meat grinder from the floor and I think that must have tumbled on him one way or another, that's what I think, but I didn't see it."

Jennie Olsen's and Swan Nicholson's depositions agree with Belle's statements. Both witnesses reported what they had observed and what Belle had told them that evening. When the coroner asked Swan Nicholson, "Do you think that that sausage grinder falling from where it did, hitting him on the head could have broken his skull?" Swan replied, "I think it could have possibly, but I never thought there was anything else but the way she told me." And his response to the question "Do you think it possible that she might have killed him?" was "No, I never thought so, no sir. If there had been the least trouble we should have known it, but we never heard not the least word, and they be like a couple of children, and the same as the day they were married."[1]

Coroner Bowell reported, after examining the body and hearing the evidence, that Peter Gunness had come to his death by "the accidental falling of the augur part of a sausage mill falling from the heating shelf of the cook stove in his kitchen and striking him on the back of the head." Official report to the contrary, unofficial reports have circulated in LaPorte for decades that Belle killed

Peter with the sausage grinder. (Some narratives give the weapon as a meat cleaver or a cast-iron frying pan.)

Though Jennie Olsen's official statements agreed with Belle's, Stewart Holbrook records the tradition that "a youngster of LaPorte recalled having heard little Myrtle Sorensen, Belle's daughter, remark that 'Mama brained Papa with an ax. Don't tell a soul'" (p. 142, n. 6). Though Swan Nicholson's official statements exonerated Belle, his wife's and son's accounts in later years presented quite another picture. Mrs. Nicholson recalled her husband's telling her that Peter Gunness's death didn't seem natural to him the moment he saw him lying on the floor. Albert remembered his father's cautioning him not to say anything or there might be trouble with Mrs. Gunness as he was telling his son how he thought Gunness seemed murdered. Albert repeated his father's statement to the crowd outside the funeral parlor enough times that "finally Pa told me to shut up and not tell anybody."

Though the coroner officially decreed the death accidental, his initial response was somewhat different, according to several oral accounts. Albert Nicholson reported that he and the coroner had come from town that night of December 16 and had hitched the horse to the rack and come in the back door. "He come in, walked over to Gunness, kneeled down there on his knees, felt Gunness all over, found that hole in the head. Nobody said a word. He got up from his knees, he brushed his hands like this [gesturing], looked at us and said, 'Here has been a murder.' Getting light. Belle said not a word."[2]

Ruth Coffeen knew the same tradition. She said that the coroner had been called out to the Gunness place and had felt there had been a murder committed but didn't say so "because on one side of the bed was the doctor. On the other side was Mrs. Gunness glaring at him." The coroner was afraid of her. Ruth's comment on the inquest findings indicates that the current unofficial tradition is the more plausible of the two for LaPorte residents: "But, anyway, Peter Gunness was killed with a meat grinder *dropping* on his head, a very likely story!"[3]

The sausage grinder, whether dropped accidentally or intentionally, was the cause of Peter Gunness's death. A kitchen utensil, an implement of hearth and home, became a weapon that separated husband and wife and gave the wife considerable insurance premiums. This metaphorical use of the grinder is expressed in several residents' humorous comments about marital relationships. Louis Blake, for example, remembered his mother-in-law, "whenever things got going at home, whenever she got provoked" at her husband, saying, "Be careful, a meat grinder might fall on your head!" Another resident has a chopping block which is said to have come from the Gunness home. It was given to her by a former husband, upon whom she said that she had been tempted to use it for the same reason as old Belle had. Marital tensions accumulate within the Victorian domestic sphere.

Harold W. Poe's play *Gnista*, produced by the LaPorte High School Players in 1966 and again by the LaPorte Players Workshop in 1973, grounds the murderess's act in her motivation to surmount economic and sexual domination. The play, loosely based on the episode presented above, is set back in the 1890s on a Swedish immigrant farm in Indiana. Act 1 presents just cause for the inarticulate farm woman Belle to kill her first husband, Sven, with a heavy cast-iron skillet in an unpremeditated act. It opens with the wife holding an interior monologue with her inner self (Idgo) while she responds submissively to her husband's ugly comments. When he demands, "When I talk, you listen. I got rights here. I'm to get respect in my home," she says nothing to him, but to herself: "Ours, Sven. Not mine. Not yours. Ours." When he tells her, "We got no time for tea an' cakes" in response to her plea to invite church folk into the parlor, she remains silent but remembers: "We had a fine proper wedding. In the church with friendly people . . . . *But he took my money. He took all of my money from my trunk. He took it.* [Emphasis added] 'Your dowry,' he said. 'Your dowry for us,' he said. And he took it and I did not see it again."

By act 2, the farm woman's just desire to share property equally with her husband has blossomed into an insatiable craving for sexual and economic domination. Her second husband remarks on their wedding day, "Now, I can be my own employer working on my own farm." His statement, mirroring Sven's, Belle's first husband's, elicits her explosive "*Your* own farm?" while her inner self responds in the primal scream "*Mine!* Man takes *mine!*" His death soon follows, and the audience is led to believe his will not be the last.[4]

This imaginative reconstruction of Mrs. Gunness's motivations in killing husbands and would-be suitors is plausible, because most of her subsequent victims were well-to-do Norwegian farmers—not all of them from Minnesota, however—who understood the economic partnership implied in the advertisements she placed in the Norwegian-language newspaper *Skandinaven*:

WANTED—A WOMAN WHO owns a beautifully located and valuable farm in first class condition, wants a good and reliable man as partner in the same. Some little cash is required for which will be furnished first-class security.[5]

The sausage grinder, as the probable murder weapon in Peter Gunness's death, gained a certain notoriety of its own. Its prominence at the May 29, 1908 auction at the Gunness place is one of Gene McDonald's favorite stories. He reminisced one afternoon with Ruth Tallant, curator of the Historical Society Museum:

Gene: But they had a sausage grinder that she killed Gunness with. That was the darndest thing I ever seen. A Polish woman bought that. Well, I wouldn't of ever ate no more sausages—
Ruth: You're letting your imagination run free, Gene.
Gene: Ya, but you don't know what else she'd run through it.
Ruth: [Teasing Gene] Scald it, what's the difference?
Gene: It's a Polish woman bought that. My brother-in-law, he says, "Jesus, what you gonna do with that?" [Speaking with Polish accent] "That's all right. I wash it all off."[6]

Through the medium of the sausage grinder, Gene associated the death of Peter Gunness with the death of subsequent suitors, implying that they had all been run through the machine and ground up. Gene had picked up on the metaphor of power talked about by almost everyone in LaPorte. Henry Johnson recalled walking into the buggy shed/morgue on the Gunness farm and seeing the disinterred bodies laid out on wooden planks: "And I was completely covered with human meat. I bet there was twenty, twenty-five bodies on there." Glenn Ott referred to a photograph of the bodies in the shed and said, "And here's some of the meat they dug up! Hamburger!"

George Heusi gave the only personal-experience narrative of men-into-meat, one which he had learned from his cousin Anne Diesslin. Anne had been invited to eat with the girls at the Gunness house sometime before her father and Belle had their falling out (pp. 46–49):

The oldest girl was to go to the basement to bring up fruit. She brought up a jar with what looked like meat in it. She got holy heck from Mrs. Gunness and had to go down and bring up the right fruit jar. Anne never went back. When she found out later what happened, she figured the girl had got in the wrong part of the basement, and brought up part of the bodies in the fruit jars.[7]

"The wrong part of the basement" in George's story corresponds to oral traditions that Belle had a "walk-in" or "stand-up" butcher shop in the forbidden room discussed in chapter 4.

> That she was stronger than a man
> Her neighbors all did own;
> She butchered hogs right easily,
> And did it all alone.
>
> But hogs were just a side line,
> She indulged in now and then;
> Her favorite occupation
> Was a-butchering of men.
>
> To keep her cleaver busy
> Belle would run an ad,
> And men would come a-scurrying
> With all the cash they had.
>
> Now some say Belle killed only ten,
> And some say forty-two.
> It was hard to tell exactly,
> But there were quite a few.[8]

These ballad stanzas set up a correspondence between Belle's treatment of hogs and her treatment of men, which is extended in the folk art about her grinding up victims. One tradition has Belle chop up her victims for hog slop. By turning the men into refuse to be eaten and digested by her pigs, she has made them a structural part of the hogpen. Another tradition has her make men into sausage and sell it to LaPorte customers or ship it to Chicago markets. In either case, she has turned men into hogs; she has become "the mail-order Circe."

Both traditions exist in a dialectic of belief within the community. Fred Hoffman has said that the shed now on his property had been "the original slaughter place where she had murdered her victims and fed them to the hogs, the pigs." Randy Hopkins, agreeing with Gene McDonald, said that he didn't like the thought of Belle's hamburgers. "A lady was sitting in the restaurant eating one day. She bit in and found her husband's ring in a hamburger. He had been missing for about three months. They found a lot of skeletons, too [in the meat she sold]."⁹

Other people are not so certain of Belle Gunness's activities. Raymond Cox, Jr. qualified his statements about "the Queen of the Abattoir": "She had a slaughter house at the farm which *undoubtedly* helped in her disposing of the some 42 victims she had *supposedly* cut up and buried about the farm. *It has been said* that she fed the flesh to her hogs." Jerry Snyder had once heard a man from out of town talk about the murderess. Although the man had exaggerated the number of her victims, Jerry said, "I just let him go on, because he said she'd killed 'em and fed 'em to the hogs. Well, *partly that is true*. She did feed parts to the hogs."¹⁰

And others discredited these folk traditions. Maxine Ford responded to my question "What about the sausage stories?" by saying, "Oh, that! I really don't believe the sausage stories, but she did raise hogs. And she did sell sausage. To a lot of people in LaPorte" [Laughing]. She continued, "Of, course, immediately when it was found out that it was a murder farm and there was a butcher and a lock-up, a stand-up locker in the basement of the home, the sausage market dropped!" Maxine concluded by reiterating her disbelief: "I really don't believe that. People were taking no more chances, though. They had it. There were some who actually were ill just thinking what they might have been eating!"¹¹

And Martin Barlag responded by giving a plausible explanation for this local manifestation of a very ancient story: "That's not true. She used lye. She didn't make sausage out of people. I can tell you how that story started. She had a big tub or vat made out of a trunk of a tree. She used that to dismember bodies to handle more easily, although she was a big, strong woman. Two hundred fifty-pound person. She could rassle with a man."¹²

The folk dialectic emerges most clearly in an argument recorded between husband and wife Jake and Susie Jones, a couple in their late twenties:

Jake: Exaggerate about the pigs, sausage stuff.
Susie: Since I was little, I heard she ground them up and fed them to hogs, sold it. Don't know whether or not they had hamburger then or not. Sold it and fed it to the pigs.
Jake: All exaggeration.
Susie: John [their son] heard at school she made hamburger.

Jake: There's been other events like Belle Gunness's. Other murders. Why do you think they keep bringing up Gunness?

Susie: Because it's a woman. In those days, women just didn't murder people, chop up people, and feed them to the hogs—.

Jake: She didn't do all that. Each generation exaggerates. Probably like a fish story. Gets bigger. If you've been raised on a farm all your life—[shrugs shoulders, implying that only city folk who know so little about hogs would think they would eat people].[13]

Whatever peoples' attitudes towards these stories, the underlying metaphorical equation men = hogs is a significant one. People seem to be talking, again, about Belle's power to create *anomie*. By transforming her victims into pigs, Belle deprived them not only of their physical identity but of their socioeconomic identity as men as well. Buried in pieces in the hog lot, possibly eaten by pigs and sold as sausages, they were nameless and unidentifiable. The elaboration of their number (e.g., ten, twelve, twenty-five, thirty, and forty-two) indicates that they had become numberless nonentities.

In a seminal 1964 article, "Anthropological Aspects of Language: Animal Categories and Verbal Abuse," Edmund Leach develops a system for looking at several cultures' pejorative associations between men and animals. It begins to explain the power these cycles of stories have in LaPorte. Leach first correlates the classification of animals (pets through wild animals) with their acceptability as a food source. Whether an animal is edible or not depends on its perceived distance from the human agent—a pet being less edible than a game animal, for instance. He then correlates the classification of relatives and friends with their perceived marriage potential. Whether a person is marriageable or not also depends on his or her distance from the agent. Leach next compares the first set of relationships to the second set. The former then becomes a metaphor for the latter.[14] The following diagram, adapted from Leach, places the metaphorical statements of the sausage stories within the context of these equivalencies.

Animal Category	: Food Source	:: Kinship	: Marriage Potential
1. game animal	edible when sexually intact	neighbors/ friends	marriage expected
2. farm animals (hogs included)	edible when castrated	cousins	marriage prohibition but premarital sex tolerated

When wealthy immigrant farmers answered Belle's matrimonial ads, they expected to be married. Like the animals in the first category, the suitors were "fair game" and thought that Belle was the same. When Mrs. Gunness turned her suitors into sausage or hog slop, she moved them into the second category of the barnyard. The hog label corresponds to the kinship category "cousin," which is, in fact, the label Belle is said to have used in introducing her numerous visitors to townspeople they met in various public places. Belle's greatest criminal act was to make these men unsuitable as husbands!

THE BLOODY MILLER

Lest the economic implications of Belle as Circe pass the reader by, a comparison to other variants of the "Bloody Miller" tale is in order. A husband characteristically butchers his wives, one by one, smokes the meat, runs it through his sausage mill, and sells human sausage for great profit in stories gathered from the Ozarks, Mississippi, Michigan's Upper Peninsula, and Wisconsin. Perhaps the most famous sausage mill belongs to "Mister Dunderbeck" or "Johnny Verbeck," who in the songs of those names is appropriately ground up in his own mill and fed to his hogs as punishment for exploiting his wives in such a way.[15]

Belle Gunness reverses this American folktale pattern. As Ann Jones states, she is first and foremost an entrepreneur who is ambitious and thoroughly American. "Using sex and property to attract her victims, Belle reversed at one stroke the familiar tales of young ladies despoiled by the vile seducer and powerless women manipulated by the man of property" (pp. 137-38). Her request that suitors bring her their money is just the reverse of the dowry system that has characterized patriarchal western societies for centuries and was the American Victorian ideal. Her request that they sell all their property is just the reverse of the legal sanctions against brides' keeping real estate in their own names, in force until the implementation of the Married Woman's Property Act. (Faragher notes that Indiana had amended the common law with regard to married women's property rights by 1861, but that implementation was piecemeal.)[16]

Belle Gunness's business acumen in converting marriage to an assembly-line production (remember Henry Johnson's "Then she'd advertise for *another* man!") sexually inverts a peculiarly Ameri-

can merger of love and money—the system of mail-order brides—
historically practiced in frontier and immigrant settlements and
currently operating through a wide network of American and
foreign connections. This system, in turn, although antithetical to
the romantic ideal for courtship and marriage, illuminates the economic aspects of marriage as men's exchange of women for goods
and property.[17]

Faragher points out that Midwestern agricultural families, much
like their peasant forebears, clearly saw the economic necessity of
marriage for both partners, at least until the mid-nineteenth century, when developing capitalism divided the workplace from the
home, and the Victorian concept of separate spheres for men and
women developed as a corollary.[18] Within this later cultural setting, marriage did become a woman's only business. As an immigrant serving-girl, it is possible that Belle understood too well that
marriage was a business arrangement and the only way up the
economic ladder in a land where the streets were not paved with
gold. She turned back to farming, where the economic components
of a marriage were still articulated, and openly advertised herself
and her land to Norwegian men whose world view was still agricultural. At the same time, she was successful in overlaying the
essential economic structure of marriage with the rhetoric of romance by which Victorians and post-Victorians hid certain
realities from each other. Storytellers talking about her making
husbands into sausage seem to be aware of the split between economics and romantic ideology which ultimately crumbled the Victorian structure.

Jones sees that the murderess simply transferred the cutthroat
tactics of business to the domestic world when she butchered men.
She effectively blurred those ideal boundaries that separated the
private domain from the public marketplace in the late nineteenth
century. Her marriage-and-murder racket was simply "the ripened
fruit" of the matrimonial agencies, the lonely hearts' clubs, and, by
extension into the present, the computer date-match organizations
"coining Cupid's wiles," as turn-of-the-century detective Clifton
Wooldridge called their activities. Chicago authorities were
prompted to stage a Progressive campaign against the proprietors
of such agencies, yet they had no way to deal with all the social
actions which were fusing those ideal spheres.[19]

Elaine May writes in *Great Expectations* that "nothing did more to shake the foundations of Victorianism than the influx of women into the labor force. Working women posed a direct challenge to the traditional sex roles which had provided the basis for domestic life." She goes on to suggest the far-reaching consequences of this change in the labor force: "Any deviation from this formula [separate spheres] threatened the entire fabric of the social order, which rested on the centrality of the family. But as more and more women went to work, the sharp separation that had divided the sexes in the nineteenth century began to break down" (pp. 115–16). Most women broke the sex barrier by moving out into the marketplace; Belle Gunness did so by pulling the marketplace into her home.

In either case, the transition into modern life was filled with tensions, (need it be said?) particularly for men. May develops this argument in the chapter "Pressure to Provide." She shows that men's roles underwent a subtle transformation that complemented that of women's as the industrial system matured. Men were ultimately caught in a double bind: the developing corporate system gave them some job security without much chance of reaching the top of the hierarchy at just the time that increased affluence and consumer spending built up expectations of increased financial support. The disjunction was apparent for white-collar workers and acute for blue-collar workers. May found that more and more divorces in her sample came about because of issues surrounding money. Many divorcing wives were not satisfied with their husbands' income, for it did not meet their aspirations for social status, an expectation built into the economic structure. She even finds evidence that it was unofficially accepted in the court system that a woman had a right to marry for money, although the official ideology, of course, was that she should marry for love.[20] So Belle Gunness's marriage for profit, at the expense of slaughtered husbands, was no longer an inversion of the system, but its apogee.

The continued popularity of the sausage stories seems to lie in these double social contexts. Belle as sausage maker both symbolically inverts the Victorian exploitation of wives and sympathetically reveals the symbolic castration of modern men, so is satisfactory from both viewpoints.

Yet the chaos in Mrs. Gunness's private domain had other public repercussions for the town of LaPorte. When she turned her hog lot into an unmarked burial ground, it became part of the town's system for dealing with its dead. William Lloyd Warner, after extensive study of Yankee City burial plots, wrote that the cemetery "as a collective representation repeats and expresses the social structure of the living as a symbolic replica; a city of the dead, it is a symbolic replica of the living community."[21] If this interpretation can be applied to the LaPorte situation, then the city's reburial of those victims not identified or claimed by relatives was an attempt to reorder the community after the Gunness upheaval. The attempt was not entirely successful.

All the victims were consigned to the pauper sections of the graveyards and so retained their marginal status. Gretchen Tyler, an officer in LaPorte's Pioneer Cemetery Association, said that some victims had to be reburied in pieces—an arm one day, a leg the next—as body parts could not be matched with certainty. She has studied turn-of-the-century sexton Abraham Bowen's cemetery log. He meticulously noted different dates for the burial of different body parts. It is said that "One leg of Andrew Helgelien" is one such entry.[22] Asle Helgelien's choice to rebury his brother in LaPorte sent out these mixed messages: the marble headstone marked the community's upheaval ("the Gunness Horror") and its attempts to return to some semblance of normalcy ("Found by His Brother"). Yet, if the Gunness Horror does symbolize economic and social changes on many levels—the movement through the pioneer barter, the Victorian entrepreneurial, and the modern corporate systems—then a return to an ordered past cannot be entirely successful or even desirable, despite the yearning for a more intimate simplicity in the exchange of goods.

If Belle Gunness did sell human sausage to people in LaPorte and Chicago, then her grisly produce became part of the town's market system. Its buyers and sellers could no longer be innocent bystanders but would be implicated in her actions as unwitting consumers of flesh. She would have turned townspeople into cannibals. People eating together has been the archetypical sign of traditional family and community togetherness; people eating each other can be an appropriate enough sign of the modern corporate world. "It's a dog-eat-dog world" and "It's a rat race" are two other animal metaphors, repeated so often that they are commonplaces, that have said the same thing.

† 6 †

BELLE GUNNESS IS ALIVE AND WELL

LaPorte Argus-Bulletin reporter Harry Darling was also a "stringer," or local correspondent, for several large metropolitan newspapers. Paid by the word for his copy, he would first telegraph a summary of the local news item to the editor's office and request how many words the final article should be before he "fired" the story. Forbes Julian, managing editor of the *Herald-Argus* from 1925 to 1965, said that Darling, who excelled at "stringer stories" that were "mostly fiction" anyhow, was known in newspaper circles as "the Biggest Telegraph Liar in the West." Bob Coffeen, who had worked with Darling, said that "as a stringer, if the news was a bit dull, he would not be above making up a story!" When the Gunness case broke, Darling was elated at firing a really big headliner to city papers. Bob Coffeen said that he sent this telegram to New York: "'22 murder victims (or whatever the number was) found on LaPorte farm. How many words?'" Bob said, "The reply was very terse, to the point, the point was well made: "Not one, you damn liar!'" This understandable unwillingness on the city editor's part to suspend disbelief did not daunt Darling in the least. According to George Heusi, he went on to write about "the phantom train" which came to view the Murder Farm.[1]

These accounts, linking the incredibility of the Gunness murders with that of Harry Darling's reporting, introduce the question of

118

media manipulation in the perception and discussion of the gruesome event in LaPorte, already implied in the first chapter of this
book. Mary Swenson exclaimed, "Oh, the reporters had a field
day!" When asked if the newspapers played it up too much, she
responded, "Of course they did. They always do. Did you ever see
any paper that they didn't? Yes, I think you can believe about half
what the newspapers say."[2] Reporters, in fact, were guilty of publishing a pseudo-love letter from Belle to Andrew Helgelien and a
photograph of a wringer washing machine as the notorious sausage
grinder.

When Forbes Julian said that the Gunness case was "right up
Darling's alley" because it was "mostly conjecture," he shifted the
problem away from newspaper manipulation to the much more
complex question of what really happened on the Gunness place in
the early morning of April 28, 1908. The proverbial saying "One
man's guess is as good as another's" makes newspapermen's specu-
lations as good as townspeople's. In fact, there is some evidence
that Darling, and the long chain of reporters after him, accurately
reflected as well as influenced their readers' various interpretations of the "true" story.

On the day that the charred bodies of a decapitated woman and
three children were found in the basement of the Gunness home,
Darling reported both the official and the unofficial guesses on the
cause of the fire. The official version ran as follows: "The officers
have only circumstantial evidence upon which to work with the
theory that possibly a former hired hand, who had been discharged,
unfriendly relations existing, had set fire to the house through a
motive of revenge." This reference was to Ray Lamphere, who was
subsequently arrested. The unofficial versions were numerous:

> This has been a day of rumors. They have been innumerable, but
> when traced were found to be without basis. One was to the effect that
> Mrs. Gunness had gone to South Bend, but the fact that she was in
> town last evening quickly disproved this report. Another is that a
> weakened mentality furnished the motive of self destruction, and that
> she planned the fire that the lives of herself and children might pay
> the penalty of her madness. [*Argus-Bulletin*, April 28, 1908]

At this point, Darling concluded that the law officers' theory of
Lamphere's incendiarism was the most logical conclusion. Com-

munity order had been disrupted, but equilibrium would be attained through the due process of law occasioned by Lamphere's arrest. Darling relegated "those who believe that despondency of the woman caused her to plan and execute the harrowing tragedy" to the category of rumormongers. If Belle had set the fire as an act of suicide, no legal action could be taken. The rumors were disorienting, for they implied that the law would be powerless to implement its sanctions.

A week later, however, when the dismembered bodies were discovered in the back lots, Darling labeled both official and unofficial guesses as "theories." His perception of Belle Gunness had made a quantum leap from "supposed victim" to "woman with more bestial than human nature," which allowed him to give more credence to the unofficial accounts of community disorder. On May 5 he wrote, "Persons are this afternoon advancing the theory that the four bodies dug from the debris last Tuesday morning were not those of Mrs. Gunness and her three children, that bodies were brought here for incineration and that Mrs. Gunness and her children, in possession of the money of her victims, sought safety in flight."

Theories of Belle's escape implied more than possible ineffectiveness on the part of the community law enforcers. They pointed to real ineptness. People have asked themselves how a woman could murder men over a period of six years and escape so neatly without the authorities' knowledge. By the time Darling reported two days later that "Coroner Mack, it is said, will officially declare that the three Gunness children were first murdered before the house was fired," he indicated that the "Belle Gunness Is Alive and Well" theory was becoming more of a logical conclusion than it had been. If she could have disposed of her children, she could just as easily have done away with another woman, whose body was left as a decoy in the burning farmhouse while she fled. Darling wrote, "Mrs. Gunness is somewhere in the flesh. Rid of her children, she found safety in flight. This is theorizing which persons conversant with the tragedy say will be substantiated with developing events" (*Argus-Bulletin*, 5 May 1908). This position was supported by the *Argus-Bulletin* from this date. Its rival, the *LaPorte Herald-Chronicle*, maintained the position that Belle had died in the fire set by her jealous handyman.

This newspaper dialectic mirrored the debate which had become not so much official versus unofficial but a problem discussed both in courts of law and by people in the street. Glen Ott said that those watching the bodies unearthed in the yard "had different ideas on it, you know, and, oh, oh, some of 'em thought she was dead there, but I couldn't never get it through my head why her head burnt up and the kids' didn't." It was just this question of the missing head which became pivotal both in the inquest held over the body supposed to be Belle Gunness's and in Ray Lamphere's trial.[3]

Coroner Charles S. Mack conducted the inquest from April 29 through May 13. The official document itself reflects the conflict. Up through May 1, the depositions of witnesses read: "Over the dead body of Belle Gunness who was supposed to have come to her death by burning. . . ." After May 5, when her victims' bodies were discovered, the depositions read: "Over the dead body of an un-identified adult female who was supposed to have come to her death by unknown cause."

In order for the coroner to establish identity of the headless body, LaPorte authorities planned a search of the Gunness property for the missing skull or jawbone with teeth. Ex-gold prospector Louis Schultz was hired to set up his sluicing equipment on the site of the farmhouse and sift through the ashes for evidence. Cheered on by thousands, Schultz made a discovery on the morning of May 19, headlined in the *Argus-Bulletin: "TEETH OF MRS. GUNNESS FOUND BY MINER SCHULTZ."* The subheading read: "Dr. I. P. Norton Makes Identification Complete and Strong Evidence Is Thus Adduced That Murderess Perished in the House."

Although Darling reported "a doubting Thomas" who asked the county sheriff: "What's to prevent Mrs. Gunness having removed her teeth and thrown them into the fire before she left," the evidence was sufficient for Coroner Mack to wind up the inquest with this statement: "It is my verdict that the body so viewed is that of Belle Gunness; that she came to her death through felonious homicide, and that the perpetrator thereof is to me unknown." The inquest report was filed in the county clerk's office on May 20.[4]

The coroner's verdict did not lay Belle Gunness to rest, however. The back jacket of *The Mrs. Gunness Mystery* suggested the under-current of belief:

$4,000.00
Reward
for the Capture Alive
of
Belle Gunness
the Sorceress of
Murder Farm
who
slew 35 persons
READ THIS BOOK!

The dialectic surfaced all the more strongly in the November 9–25, 1908 circuit court case *The State of Indiana* v. *Ray Lamphere*. Since the verdict of guilty for four counts of murder and one count of arson depended, naturally, on whether or not Belle Gunness perished in the fire, that became the central issue in the court proceedings. The state, represented by prosecuting attorney R. N. Smith and his counsel, Sutherland, attempted to establish Belle's death in the fire beyond a reasonable doubt. Conversely, the lawyer for the defense, H. W. Worden, and his counsel, Weir, attempted to establish evidence for Belle's escape from the fire. The November 26 verdict of "guilty of arson" was considered a technical victory for the state. Gene McDonald is just one of many residents, however, who labeled the trial a compromise. The jury could not accept "beyond a reasonable doubt" that Belle was dead or, if dead, had not killed herself, so the indictments of murder were dropped against Lamphere.[5]

Both journalists and legislators can be seen as "symbol specialists" who were adept at dramatizing a community's conflicts. The debate whether Belle Gunness was alive or not, expressed in rival newspaper coverage and in the court drama of Lamphere's trial, did reflect the political dialectic in LaPorte at the time. On the one hand, the *LaPorte Herald-Chronicle* offices, the sheriff of LaPorte County, and the prosecuting attorneys for Lamphere's trial supported the statement that Belle Gunness was dead—and all were Republican. On the other hand, the *LaPorte Argus-Bulletin* and the defense attorneys for Lamphere's trial supported the statement that Belle Gunness was alive—and all were Democratic. The two-party political system was symbolically represented in the narratives' bipartisan structure.

The Gunness story, however, is more deeply involved in the community's political structure. Stories about Belle's escaping the fire to enjoy her wealth are the ones told most often in LaPorte today. They extend the implication that the town's law officers were inept to the suggestion that they were accomplices in Belle's crimes. Inferences of their collusion range from the sheriff's part in helping the murderess escape to a major conspiracy to set Ray Lamphere up as a dupe involving cover-ups on the parts of coroner, lawyers, judge, jurors, and professional men in LaPorte. The road from political bickering to conspiracy will be traced in the wanderings of the murderess after her supposed death by burning.

MRS. GUNNESS VERY NUMEROUS

Although the *Herald-Chronicle* derisively labeled reports of Gunness sightings after the fire as "Mrs. Gunness Very Numerous," several personal-encounter narratives deserve detailed attention. One of the first sightings was on July 9, 1908, by Belle's neighbor Daniel Hutson and his daughters Eldora and Evaline. His story, reported in the local press, was largely dismissed until he was called as a witness for the defense at Lamphere's trial, his daughters giving corroborating evidence. The *Argus-Bulletin* reporter covering the case, probably Darling, gave a contextual description of his testimony. The setting is a packed courtroom close to the end of the trial. The narrator, under oath, is speaking to several different audiences: to the judge and jurors as community guardians and upholders of the law and to the courtroom audience as the public.

The reporter gives this text:

Hudson's [Hutson's] story is that he was driving in the road on a hayrack when he saw through the trees Mrs. Gunness and the man walking in the orchard on the Gunness place. "Even at that distance I could recognize her plainly," said Hudson. "I knew her size, I knew her shape and I knew her lumbering walk. I never saw another woman who walked like her. I started my horses to try to get up the hill to the orchard before she could get away, but she saw me first and she and the man ran to the buggy, clambered in and raced straight to the main road. I was within twenty feet of her at one time and could plainly see her face, although she wore a double veil—a black veil over a white one. It was Mrs. Gunness and no one else; I am positive of that.

The reporter then described the coming to the stand of nine-year-old Eldora and twelve-year-old Evaline. They both testified that they had seen Mrs. Gunness and the man riding in a buggy down the road and had told their father so before he had told them of his experience. The reporter concluded with a description of the audience's reaction: "The testimony of Hudson and his girls was strangely received by the spectators. The court room audience is divided in sentiment; part believing Mrs. Gunness to be dead, and the rest equally positive she is alive" (*Argus-Bulletin*, 23 November 1908).

Eldora Hutson Burns filled out the immediate contextual situation almost seventy years later. She said that the defense lawyers had asked her preliminary questions on the stand. "First thing they asked me if I knew what the truth was. And I told them yes. And then they asked me what would happen if I didn't tell the truth and I told them, 'The evidence wouldn't be any good.'" Worden and Weir then asked her if anyone had primed her before she had come to the stand. When she said that, yes, her father had told her what to say, there was an audible gasp in the courtroom. "They asked what he told me, and I told them telling me to tell the story I knew and nothing more. And I needn't be afraid to talk to nobody."

Eldora also filled in the broader political context. Although her father had told her she "needn't be afraid to talk to nobody," their farm was under surveillance from the time Daniel Hutson first reported seeing Belle alive until long after the family had been on the witness stand. "Well, I was awful nervous for a little girl," she remembers. "There were so many detectives and everything around the place. Day and night, anytime, they'd be around the house. Someone listening to what you said." She told me that her father "kinda began to suspect that some of the people that were supposed to be on the side of the law were mixed up with Belle" and were keeping an eye on the Hutsons, as well as secretly probing the Gunness orchard for the wealth possibly buried there.

Despite this threat, Eldora always told the "story she knew," as her accounts, recorded in 1952 and in 1976, are almost verbatim. In both these recording sessions, Eldora speaks of her mother's doubting the rest of the family's experiences. She told Lillian de la Torre that her mother said, "You're daffy, you've heard so much," and she told me, "Our mother told us, oh, we must be mistaken, she was dead." The conflict in the courtroom audience has been transferred to the story itself, as Eldora's current audience, her son Glen, daughter-in-law Elsie, and grandson Keith, have already been persuaded that Belle escaped the fire. When I asked if Belle lived, they all said yes, although Elsie added, "She's too old to be alive any more."[6]

Eldora's guess that Belle had returned "to look for something up in that orchard" is matched by John Nepsha, Jr.'s story. His family had not yet built their home on the Gunness property in 1923, but they were using the land for pasture. It was his chore, and he was seven or eight years old at the time, to bring their twelve cows in for milking and then return them to the pasture. He continued:

> And one morning I took them out there and, closing the gate, I noticed a fresh hole dug. So I ran home and told Dad and Mother about it. They both come out. I went with them. And there was a hole dug on the west corner from the house about twenty feet by an apple tree. It was an old apple tree, but there was a new sprout coming out. And the shape, the bottom of the hole, was like a little trunk, oh, I'd say about two feet by eighteen inches, something like that [John demonstrated by shaping his hands into a rectangle]. Was taken out of there. And footprints on the fresh soil was a man's prints and a woman's prints.[7]

Although this event occurred fifteen years after the fire and gives only indirect evidence that Belle had returned with an escort, John said that "Mother always said that she probably had her silverware in there" and had come to retrieve it. The political implications of this account are more indirect, also. John prefaced his story with this comment: "My folks never reported it either. They should have." And he concluded his story, "My Dad and Mother should have reported that to the sheriff but, see, they never did." Why the Nepshas never told this experience to the authorities might be related to a statement John made a little later in our interview: "Well, actually, a lot of people say that Belle Gunness and the sheriff were together on all that stuff."

And Donald Woodford, the grandson of Asle Helgelien, still living in South Dakota as his grandfather and great-uncle had before him, shared Helgelien family stories about events in LaPorte. He said that he never had heard about the Gunness story until after he graduated from high school in 1939. He and the other children had heard family members make some reference to some tragedy or scandal, but whenever they asked for information, they were told to go out and play and not to worry about it. He explained, "We later found out that the reason for all of this secrecy was the fact that they were fearful that if Belle Gunness was still living she might still be looking for relatives of Asle Helgelien or for Asle himself so that she could get revenge. They did seem to all believe that Belle was still alive."

After he and his wife visited LaPorte in 1973 and walked out to Patton Cemetery to see Andrew's grave, Donald spoke to his mother, Asle's daughter, about those years. Only then did she tell him how the family was very bitter about the sheriff. For the sheriff and his men had treated Asle horridly. Asle had told his daughter that he was afraid that they were going to do away with him when Andrew's body was first uncovered in Belle Gunness's farmyard. And this tradition comes from the person seen as the star witness for the state.[8]

The sheriff, in an attempt to stem the flow of this tradition, gave an interview published in the *LaPorte Herald-Argus* on May 11, 1934. (The *Herald-Argus* was the nonpartisan result of the merger of the *Herald-Chronicle* and the *Argus-Bulletin* in 1924.) He had recently returned to LaPorte after some years of absence in Texas, in which, it was conjectured by some, he had spent his share of Belle's profits. In answer to the reporter's query, he said that it was his "flat opinion" that Belle and her three children had perished in the fire twenty-six years before. He gave a reason for the origin of the story of Belle's escape: "Then, one night, Al Pegler of the *Chicago American* came to me and said, 'Sheriff, I know Mrs. Gunness is dead, but I'm going to send in a story saying she didn't die in the fire, just to give the case a new angle.' When I protested he told me that I 'was a good sheriff but a poor newspaperman.'" The sheriff continued, "The next day . . . the story was spread over the entire front page of the *American*, and it was then that talk of Mrs. Gunness' escaping started. It had its origin in the mind of one newspaperman." And he gave a reason for the transmission of the story when he declared that "political enemies" had deliberately spread the story to discredit him, strongly implicating the defense lawyer, Wirt Worden, who by 1934 was a judge of the district court (*Herald-Argus* 11 May 1934).

The sheriff's counter-accusation of political muckraking was particularly leveled against the LaPorte County authorities' special consideration of reports that Belle had reappeared in California in 1931. Although they had finally dismissed most of the reports that Belle had been seen throughout the United States, they paid attention to this case. Deputy district attorney George Stahlman of Los Angeles County wrote to LaPorte sheriff Tom McDonald in the spring of 1931 that the defendant in a pending murder case might be Mrs. Gunness under an alias. Mrs. Esther Carlson, who was accused of poisoning her eighty-one-year-old charge August Lindstrom for his bank account, had in her effects pictures of children who bore a striking resemblance to Myrtle and Lucy Sorensen and Philip Gunness. Her own photograph was published next to a 1907 picture of Belle in an April 29, 1931 *Herald-Argus* article with the caption: "Are these pictures of the same woman at different ages?" The answer over the years in LaPorte has been a qualified yes.

That answer does have political overtones. Sheriff McDonald, who considered sending representatives to Los Angeles to identify the woman but could not afford to do so in the heart of the Depression, was a Democrat. He was assisted on all levels of the inquiry by Wirt Worden. Judge Worden, in a 1938 lecture to a history class at LaPorte High School, restated his belief that Belle had escaped the fire in 1908 to die, as Esther Carlson, of tuberculosis before her 1931 trial. The Historical Society booklet *The Gunness Story* contains a condensed version of his speech (pp. 7–15). Its numerous reprintings and high volume of sales have helped perpetuate in print the oral tradition. Miriam Terry's statement that "rumors began to float around that she was seen in California" represents present knowledge of this segment of the "Belle Gunness Is Alive and Well" legend.[9]

The Republican sheriff's 1934 disclaimer, designed to dispel the tradition, may have been instrumental in splintering it into another, which was ultimately more detrimental to his reputation. Charles Pahrman, a Gunness expert in the 1950s, "theorized" (to use Darling's term) that Belle had, indeed, been helped in escaping the fire, only to be killed herself immediately afterwards. He guessed her accomplices, nominally law officers, cut the teeth from her mouth, planted them in the ashes of the farmhouse so that it would appear she had died there, and then took all the spoils rather than their share. This interpretation makes political chaos complete. The law givers are doubly lawless—they aid and abet a criminal and then murder her for monetary gain.

This version entered popular as well as oral tradition with the publication of *The Truth about Belle Gunness* in 1955, as Charles Pahrman had been a major source for Lillian de la Torre's study. The following excerpt is taken from a spirited conversation among Gene McDonald, Evelyn Nordyke, and Art Flickinger, debating the Gunness case once again in the fall of 1976. Their conversation captures the community dialectic about politics and shows the interdependence of popular and oral sources used as evidence in this perennial discussion:

> Art: Gal wrote book five or six years ago [Lillian de la Torre]. Think she got as close to it as anyone . . . . I knew old Doc Antis. Sat up in his office. We talked about it. He thought, night of fire, someone done away with her. She was killed for her money.
>
> Evelyn: I don't.
>
> Gene: She got away.
>
> Art: Teeth in fire. Like she [Lillian de la Torre] said, couldn't have been torn out of her mouth unless she was dead.
>
> Evelyn: Somebody could have put them in there.
>
> Gene: [Strongly] That whole thing was baloney. I knew Belle well.
>
> Evelyn: I think she got away.
>
> Art: No, she lured another woman in [to replace her in the fire]. Got done away with herself.
>
> Gene: I don't believe it. She went to Stillwell to catch the 4:50 train [after she escaped the burning farmhouse]. I can tell you who took her. I fired with the sheriff's brother. I knew the sheriff when he was the foreman of the delivery barn. He wasn't in on it.
>
> Art: How'd the sheriff get $15,000 then?
>
> Gene: . . . I was out there [when the bodies were dug up]. Nobody can tell me the sheriff was in on it. I was there when he was digging it up. And I know damn well she got out of there.[10]

The argument has shifted; it is no longer a question whether Belle Gunness died in the fire or not, but whether her accomplices killed her soon after her escape or not. Lillian de la Torre has said that the truth is often a compromise and usually lies somewhere down the middle between the divergent positions. Her reading of the situation, that Belle did escape but was soon killed by her conspirators, is most intellectually satisfying even if most damaging to the community's sense of law and order.

Yet de la Torre wrote, directed, and took the lead in a play, entitled *The Coffee Cup*, in which the murderess gets away. In the 1952 production, Belle, under the alias Brunhilde Larson, is living in an Indiana farmhouse in 1913. When an inquisitive neighbor comments that the murderess "set that fire herself, and then she ran away. You ask anybody in LaPorte," she responds tersely, and ironically, "More silly talk. She burned up."[11]

As all the interpretations presented here are plausible given the historical mystery of the night of the fire, it is significant that the tradition that Belle lives on is the most predominant one in LaPorte today. At first glance, it appears that the Democrats have won a symbolic victory, at least. Yet at second glance, the symbolic implications of this tradition no longer are bipartisan but touch on modern concerns about the corporate structure and the government.

SHAMMING SICKNESS IN FLIGHT

In *Women Who Kill*, Ann Jones discusses the possible flight of the murderess out of LaPorte and into oblivion. On May 8, 1908, authorities arrested a wealthy widow, Mrs. Flora Belle Heerin, on her way from Chicago to New York to visit her sister. Pulled off the train in Syracuse by city police, she was detained as Belle Gunness. Although she later sued Syracuse police and train officials for false arrest, the real murderess would have had ample time to leave LaPorte unnoticed. Jones says that "she had more than a week to travel undeterred and to read in the newspapers the sad story of the death of a 'well-to-do widow' and her children in a tragic fire" (pp. 135–36).

Ray Lamphere had always maintained that he had taken her to the train station at Stillwell, Indiana after the fire was set on April 28. A cabman for Decatur, Indiana, Jesse L. Hurst, "believed he had seen Mrs. Gunness, bundled up, borne on a stretcher and shamming sickness" at the train station in Decatur the day after the fire, April 29. Cabman Hurst, as quoted in the *Mrs. Gunness Mystery*, said that "while I was standing with my hack at the depot, a man came to me and wanted me to haul a sick woman from the Erie depot to the Grand Rapids & Indiana railway station." Based on her appearance, for "she was very large, weighing about 225 pounds," and on her actions, for she "acted very strangely," Mr. Hurst assumed that the woman was using illness as a device for escape. She was carried onto a southbound train for Berne, Indiana on a stretcher (pp. 171–72).

Motifs of Belle's size and her male escort connect this story with Eldora Hutson's and John Nepsha's, discussed above. At the same time, Hurst's story is similar to Louis Blake's account, recorded in 1975, of his experience with a woman resembling Belle in 1917. Right before World War I, Louis was an ambulance driver for an undertaker who had one of the first motorized vehicles in northern Indiana. His wife-to-be, Lydia Decker, was a student nurse at Epworth Hospital (now Memorial Hospital) in South Bend. He and his partner had gotten a call and "went down and got this old lady who claimed she'd been hurt on the train." They took her to Epworth, where the doctors "examined her, could find no injury of any kind, could find nothing wrong with her, but they put her in a room." Nurse Decker went into the room. The old woman looked up at her and said, "Is your pappy still out on the farm?" As Lydia's father had sold Belle Gunness egg settings, Louis said that his wife "of course thought it was Mrs. Gunness."

By the time that "South Bend police detectives, I assume they were detectives, maybe they were just officers, came up to the hospital and said they had traced her that far," Louis said, the room was empty. The hospital staff speculated that Belle had been able to bribe Louis's ambulance partner and that "he had gotten a taxi for her and spirited her out of the hospital."

Louis prefaced his story with a question: "You're not going to record my 'lies,' are you?" The tall-tale quality of this narrative subtradition does, in fact, signal a shift in attitude towards Belle as mass murderess and towards law and order in general. Although Louis said that the LaPorte County sheriff had been accused through the years of "being in cahoots" with Belle and that that was detrimental to the community, he (as storyteller) and myself (as interviewer) had a sense of satisfaction that Old Lady Gunness had given the South Bend police the slip.[12]

As stories of her sightings place her farther and farther from LaPorte, both geographically and temporally, so she is perceived as

as much a trickster as a monster. When people in LaPorte say that
she was "too smart" to die in the fire, that she was able "to pull the
wool over everybody's eyes," and that she was a "tricky Norwegian," they are according her the mingled admiration and disgust
that tellers and audiences have displayed towards trickster figures
in the world's mythologies and folktales.[13] The legends of Belle's
deceptions and transformations in flight place her within the ranks
of American outlaws, special types of tricksters, who are feared for
their crimes yet admired for outwitting the law. LaPorteans, who
in good conscience have been unable to frame her acts within the
Robin Hood-as-social-hero mold, have associated her with the underworld heroes Al Capone and John Dillinger, who were said to
have had hideouts in northern Indiana. Someone from southern
Indiana, a resident of the town of Seymour, made this association
concrete when he said that the members of the Reno gang were
able to escape detection and arrest by concealing their stolen bank
notes in the rolls of Mrs. Gunness's fat![14] Ruth Coffeen called Belle
outlaw Sam Bass's "feminine counterpart" and modeled some of the
lyrics in her ballad after "The Ballad of Sam Bass." The last two
stanzas of the Gunness ballad connect the formal similarity of the
text with the thematic similarity of fugitive-from-justice:

> They looked for her in Texas
> In sunny Tennessee
> They sought her most from coast to coast
> O where, O where was she?
>
> Perhaps she's gone to heaven
> There's none of us can say
> But if I'm right in my surmise
> She's gone the other way.[15]

When Stewart Holbrook wrote an *American Mercury* piece about
Belle Gunness in 1941, he received a fascinating letter from a
reader, John Black (pseud.), who had had his own possible run-in
with the lady killer some years before. In 1935, Black had read an
illustrated article about Gunness in a detective magazine. The picture of the murderess haunted him, for he felt that he had seen her
face before. It came to him that she resembled the madam of a
house of prostitution in Ohio that his fraternity brothers had fre-
quented during their college years.

In a spirit of inquiry, he visited the brothel and confronted the woman, who he said was a legend throughout the state in her own right for her status outside the law. "Hello, Belle," he had said. The woman, visibly shaken, dropped a tray she was carrying and ran into the kitchen. Later, she asked him why he had called her Belle Gunness and told him that was a horrible accusation, as she remembered what the murderess had done. He then asked a fraternity brother to check into the madam's history and her possible connection to Belle Gunness. The brother came to him a week later and told him that the incident was closed and that he should forget the whole thing. Black did not forget the whole thing, but his correspondence with Holbrook ends, so that we are left with a delicious sense of the woman's elusiveness once more.[16]

Alfred Fox, a retired law officer, spent some time tracking down a 1959 "rumor" that Belle was still alive in the small community of Fish Lake, not far from LaPorte. He talked to people who were born and raised in the area, and none could say who she might be. He talked to city, county, and state police, who had only "these bits and pieces to go on, too," as she was so clever that "she didn't leave a trail." He concluded, after everyone figured out that Belle would have been at least a hundred years old, that the story had gotten out of proportion. "It was a rumored situation," he said. "It won't die. It will live around this area for as long as people talk." He ended the interview with this comment: "You know, like Jesse James is still living."[17]

Although Alfred Fox did not develop the "Jesse James Is Alive and Well" side of his comparison, it can be done. Homer Croy, in the chapter "Myths after Jesse James" in his *Jesse James Was My Neighbor*, writes that the "most persistent myth" about Jesse was that he had not been killed in Saint Joseph, Missouri in 1882. C. L. Sonnichsen and William V. Morrison found the same to be true in their study *Alias Billy the Kid*. Many people, especially old-timers who had known the Kid, felt that he was not killed by Sheriff Pat Garrett in Fort Sumner, New Mexico in 1881, but had gone on to live a law-abiding life in Old Mexico. Croy's statement about the presumed longevity of these outlaws can be applied to Belle Gunness as well. He writes, "For it would seem that the public does not want to believe that a person it has been interested in is no more."[18] That brings us back to Stewart Holbrook's observation in chapter 1

(p. 32–33) that "Belle Gunness lives on in that misty, unmapped half-world that Americans have made and lovingly preserve for certain of their folk villains."

Stories about these "badmen(women) heroes" living on are as much a statement about attitudes towards principles of order and disorder as they are about the particular tricksters who embody them. Roger Abrahams introduces his analysis of American heroes with the general statement that "hero stories are a depiction, a projection of values in story form." These projected values can be normative, in the sense that they guide those who tell them and listen to them in their actions in everyday life. Or these values can be vicarious wish-fulfillments functioning as classic "steam valves" for those who talk about heroes, villains, and rogues. Belle Gunness as trickster is an apt metaphor for expressing ambivalent feelings about law enforcement in general and for intellectually working out the relative categories of good and evil.[19]

BELLE GUNNESS, SUPERWOMAN

Evelyn Nordyke and Gene McDonald continued their conversation in the front room of the county museum in October of 1976:

Evelyn: "I think she was living."
  Gene: "I do too. She's living."
Evelyn: [Surprised] "Oh, she's dead now."
  Gene: "Maybe she ain't. Maybe she had a superlife."

Belle's "superlife" has had a long tradition in LaPorte. Its mythic realization usually rests with young people and children who never knew the historic personality. Stewart Holbrook, writing in 1941, said, "School boys and girls in the LaPorte district of thirty years ago often heard terrifying sounds issuing from the swamp near Belle's place, including cries for help, but whether with a Scandinavian accent or not, I could not learn. Many middle-aged folk today believe the swamp is haunted" (p. 241). Recent interviews with young LaPorteans indicate that modern supernatural legends are being superimposed on or generated from the community legend of the murderess. Stories about going to the site of Belle Gunness's farmhouse and of calling Belle's spirit in a seance are common. Ramona Hernandez's report is a model. She outlines the situation: LaPorte friends are having a last-fling party of the summer before returning to their respective colleges. They decide to have a seance. "Once it had become dark, I led the group into the deepest part of the woods. There we formed a circle, held hands and doused the lights." There was some discussion on whom to call back, but "since we were true and faithful LaPorteans, we followed the age-old tradition of choosing Belle Gunness as our night's celebrity."

One seance participant said that calling back Belle Gunness was not a good idea. As evidence, she told the group the story of a friend's friend who had participated in a seance where Belle's spirit had actually been contacted. The girl said, "Suddenly, one of the girls began to scream. The seance was suspended as they madly searched for the flashlights. Once they did have some light, the girl who screamed was dead with her back covered with wounds from a knife (the weapon used by Belle in her murders)." The story's effect was to cause the participants to disband and regroup for a marsh-mallow fight as safer entertainment. Ramona said that the group, "being from LaPorte, all knew the original story of Belle Gunness, giving this new story much more weight."[20]

Gerri Wallis said that "every time, you know, we had a seance, we always called Belle Gunness, John F. Kennedy, and—who else—John Kennedy. Some people called Lincoln." It is significant here that Belle Gunness has been associated with two assasinated presidents of the United States, folk and popular heroes for many Americans. There are, or have been, narrative traditions that cast doubt on the deaths of both the slain men. Lloyd Lewis, in his *Myths after Lincoln*, reports that "the principal myth" from 1865 through the 1920s was that Lincoln's tomb was empty. Bruce A. Rosenberg has analyzed similar stories about John F. Kennedy's grave, with the attendant narratives that Kennedy is still alive, as a vegetable, in an army hospital or on Onassis's Greek isle.[21]

Although Lewis for Lincoln and Rosenberg for Kennedy compare these narratives to the mythological motifs of the culture hero still living and the culture hero's expected return in a time of crisis, an underlying theme of these legends seems to be the credibility gap between official governmental pronouncements and possible real-ity. There are at least two alternate readings of the tradition seen from this light. The first suggests that the hero will return and

that good, the good of small-town values, will prevail despite pro-
liferating federal bureaucracy. The second suggests that the federal government is falsely encouraging adulation for dead heroes
while the real men lie in nonhuman states (Lincoln as petrified
stone, Kennedy as a living vegetable), victims of a massive conspiracy. In either case, the existence of good is muted by the persistence of evil in the structure of law and order itself.

The above conclusion has already been presented on the community scale in the dialectic of Belle's possible death or escape.
That Belle Gunness lives on is an appropriate symbol for a certain
uneasiness about bureaucracies, whether governmental or corporate, that plague these modern times. Current rumors and legends
circulate about the evil deeds carried on by major corporations and
manufacturers, far from the eye of the public, from Procter and
Gamble's being run by Devil-worshippers to the Big Three auto
companies' suppressing the patent for an engine that uses very little gas. They circulate about foreign substances in our food—rodent
parts, human fingers, razor blades—products of mass distribution
no longer under an individual homemaker's control. They circulate
about government conspiracies, mafioso control of political deci-
sions, and international networks of drug traffickers (none is nec-
essarily false information, it is simply not verified). All point to the
modern person's dilemma, the loss of control in an expanding universe. No one in LaPorte has named a computer after Belle Gunness, or a nuclear reactor, to my knowledge, but perhaps the time
is not far off.[22]

CONCLUSION

BRICOLAGE
RECONSIDERED

ALTHOUGH ONE CAN'T BE precisely sure what Stewart Holbrook meant when he said that Belle Gunness was assured of an enduring place in the folklore of northern Indiana, it is true that community folk art has shaped a decades-rich body of expressive culture around the local murderess and her acts.[1] The narrative pieces in the Gunness puzzle have been variously shaped and sized; some have remained relatively stable, while others have shifted through the years. The story pieces have, in fact, exhibited all the characteristics that researchers have noted for the life and death of a myth.

The transmission processes that Gordon Allport and Leo Postman have called "leveling" and "sharpening" and Gyula Ortutay "selection" are apparent within the Gunness narrative cycle.[2] The conflicting stories about Belle's house, for example, still uniformly telescope its history into that of the deviant women who lived within it. And the early-twentieth-century perception of Belle as a Victorian lady killer poisoning and bludgeoning men, women, and children scales down to the late-twentieth-century perception of Belle as a modern murderess dismembering only men.

The opposing process that Ortutay has labeled "elaboration" and Warren A. Peterson and Noel P. Gist "compounding" is also discernible and, indeed, grows out of the first.[3] Narratives about Belle

136

as a man in disguise can be read as expansions of the stories about her male clothing, strength, and occupations already marking her deviancy. Stories about the mutilation of her male victims have developed, quite logically, into the narratives that she made and sold sweet sausage from their remains. And the stories that she escaped detection to live comfortably on the proceeds of her crimes have grown, to some extent, from contradictory evidence never fully resolved, as indicated by the compromise verdict at handyman Ray Lamphere's trial.

These processes are related to another, which Ortutay has labeled "affinity," in which events under discussion act, as John Fischer notes, "as magnets which attract psychologically appropriate mythical motifs and other congruent traditional material, including historical material from other times."[4] It is true that Indiana narrators have used appropriate mythical motifs in discussing Belle Gunness's murders when they have drawn upon the tales of "Bluebeard" and "The Bloody Miller," and the motifs of "The Culture Hero Returns" and "The Strong Man" in their storytelling.

It is equally true that they have drawn upon congruent historical material in shaping their perceptions of the murderess. At the turn of the century, when Belle's crimes were fresh, people compared her to the Bender family, who had apparently murdered travelers passing through Labette County, Kansas from 1871 to 1873. The May 8, 1908 *LaPorte Argus-Bulletin* called the two cases "parallel horrors in crime." They were given concrete family connections by the *Chicago Record-Herald*, which reported on May 10, 1908 that "Mrs. Gunness [is] said to be related to the Benders." Although the Bender family were Pennsylvania German in origin and so not related to Belle Gunness genetically, their methods of murder, the discovery of their victims, and popular and folk coverage of the event were remarkably similar to those of the Gunness case.[5]

Since 1945, a few LaPorte residents have reported hearing that Belle had upholstered her kitchen chairs with the tatooed skins of her victims. Residents of Plainfield, Wisconsin heard the same about Ed Gein, a retiring farmer accused in 1957 of murdering two women and robbing the graves of many others.[6] In both cases, few neighbors had been allowed into the homes to see what they actually contained. In Belle's case, the farmhouse had burned before an official inventory could be made, so that the historical accuracy of this report cannot be verified. Yet the implicit analogy between Belle and Ilse Koch, known as "the Witch of Buchenwald," who did make lampshades out of the skins of concentration camp prisoners during the Second World War, is unavoidable.

Many LaPorte residents currently compare the Gunness murders with recent mass murders in the United States. For example, some have made reference to the Manson Family's 1969 Tate-LaBianca murders. This connection was visibly indexed in LaPorte when the words "Helter Skelter" were spray-painted across a road sign in front of what was Belle's property (and which now belongs to the Nepsha family) in 1976. "Helter Skelter," the Beatles song which Charles Manson adopted as his theme song, is an appropriate label for the community disorder encapsulated in the house on McClung Road.[7]

Soon after Juan V. Corona was arrested and charged with the mass murder of migrant workmen in California on May 26, 1971, Maxine Ray Ford wrote an article headlined "Join the Club" in the *LaPorte Herald-Argus*. The first sentence reads: "Events that transpired in recent days near Yuba City, California, in which bodies of a number of murdered men were unearthed in an orchard area rekindle the fabulous story of Belle Gunness, who made LaPorte famous or infamous whether we care to claim her or not." A little over two years later, when Dean Allen Corll was accused of killing and burying teenage boys in Houston, Texas, Maxine wrote on August 20, 1973, "Revelation of Corll's unspeakable crimes has revived interest in the record performance of LaPorte's infamous Lady Bluebeard, Belle Gunness, who gave our city the dubious distinction of being called the mass murder capital more than half a century ago." Her comparisons return to the themes articulated in the first chapter.

And younger LaPorte residents, usually those thirty and under, have compared Belle's case to the play "Arsenic and Old Lace," in which two "pixilated" old maids kill their gentlemen callers out of pity. The popularity of the 1941 play by J. O. Kesselring, its 1944 movie adaptation by Frank Capra, and its numerous high-school and community theater productions have ensured the transfer of its macabre humor to the Gunness crimes.[8] The comparison reflects just those attitudinal shifts in perceiving Mrs. Gunness as monster, as trickster, and, finally, as "Dear Old Belle."

The blending of cases seen to be analogous when discussing the Gunness crimes complements the process Allport and Postman have seen as the final one in rumor transmission. What they have called "assimilation" occurs when the content of the oral communication is "skewed in the direction of established habits and conventions," the implication being that some facts drop out of narrative if they do not conform to cultural patterns, while others are added, despite their inaccuracy, if they do so conform.[9] Within this context, the view of Belle Gunness as a "death mother," which corresponds to the Victorian sense of women's place in marriage, and the view of the murderess as a "deadly wife," which corresponds to post-Victorian marriage expectations, can be read as proofs of narrative acculturation.

From Allport and Postman's perspective, one shared by many researchers dealing with oral tradition, once the tradition becomes embedded in the sociocultural matrix of its tellers and listeners, the information so transmitted is unreliable historically and, therefore, not valid data. Although it is not my intention here to recapitulate the debate on the veracity of orally transmitted information, it is worth noting that Richard Dorson has written in one of his essays in *American Folklore and the Historian* that shared beliefs of a community, whether found to be true or false, are themselves historical facts worth documenting. And social historians Robert Darnton and John Mack Faragher have found the analysis of folk traditions to be one of the few ways a researcher can enter the *mentalité*s of everyday people.[10] From this second perspective, the transmission processes discussed above become the basis for reading the *significance* of a tradition rather than its distortion.

And the Gunness story is significant when it is perceived, as all folk art can be, as a powerful tool in constructing meaning on a social level. Victor Turner's analysis of historical events' developing into metaphors within a society is a useful way of looking at the Belle Gunness phenomenon, and one that underlies the approach built up in the preceding chapters. For Turner, the first step in the group process of creating metaphor, what he calls a social drama, depends on a publicly recognized breach in social relations within a community.[11] The discovery of the mass murders in 1908 was such a recognition. At that time, and for years afterwards, LaPorte townspeople acknowledged that their local murderess had literally inverted all the codes of behavior that their community traditionally sanctioned. As we have seen, she not only violated the ethical and moral code of valuing human life, she also broke the codes of hospitality, neighborliness, gender identity, marriage, and kinship, and of business and political ethics, as well.

The second step, and perhaps the most important one for the discussion here, Turner has labeled "crisis." At this point in the process, the community sees the initial breach as coextensive with major cultural conflicts and, in so doing, makes that event a metaphor of cultural disjunction. Turner's crisis model suggests that the event becomes invisible in itself as it is turned into a vehicle for group understanding of the cultural processes in disorder around them.[12] As I have attempted to show in previous chapters, the Gunness Horror does disappear for townspeople as it becomes a complex sign of traditional community breakdown in the face of urban shifts. Here the figure of Belle Gunness symbolically inverts the old values while representing the new in their most anxiety-producing forms.

The third step in the social drama Turner has called "redress." In this stage, the community attempts through legal action to remedy wrongs or grievances presented in the crisis situation. The resulting fourth step is either a reintegration of cultural oppositions or a social recognition of cultural schism.[13] That Belle Gunness was never brought to trial and that Ray Lamphere's trial was so inconclusive indicate that the redressive action was not successful on the literal level: the murderess did not receive her just deserts. And on the symbolic level, the cultural schism remains as well. As the Park Dixon Goist quote in the introduction intimates, the dialectic over the image of community, balanced between the small town and the big city, remains a major issue of American cultural life in the twentieth century, as it was in the nineteenth. The Gunness story's persistence through change for over seventy-five years indicates that the cultural matrix out of which it grows–the conflicting image of community in an increasingly urbanized landscape–is still in crisis. And so, from this viewpoint, the Gunness story has been articulated and will be rearticulated until that cultural issue is resolved.

In her play *The Coffee Cup*, Lillian de la Torre pits a lady crime-writer, Miss Palliser, against the murderess posing as the farmwoman Brunhilde Larson. Soon after Miss Palliser correctly identifies Mrs. Larson as Belle Gunness, the detective writer switches coffee cups with Belle when she suspects that Belle is trying to poison her. On her last gasp, she finds that she has made a fatal mistake: Mrs. Gunness was going to kill herself, so that the too-clever detective writer drank the poison instead. In writing of her play, de la Torre said, "My detective is a lady crime-writer because I am a lady crime-writer. I wish I could have made a better detective."[14]

It has been good to keep de la Torre's self-reflexive irony in mind as I have worked with the Belle Gunness material. The hypothesis presented here–that folk art about the murderess signifies complex community attitudes towards modernization, urbanization, industrialization, and, finally, the corporate system–is only one of various interpretations possible for why people have talked about the "Lady Bluebeard" so many years after her crimes were committed. Some of the steps towards that conclusion will be reviewed here before the implications of this study can be explored. First, as a folklorist trained in folk narrative theory and field research methods, I was fairly certain that the Gunness narratives were still current because they were something more than entertaining, (although they certainly are that) even before I began my field study in LaPorte. My interview questions were originally planned with the murders as the specific focus. Yet, after listening to peoples' interview answers and to more informal conversations, I found that they wanted to talk about Belle Gunness's deviancy on all social levels. This generalizing tendency was true for other field researchers' findings as well.

These field data led me to the second step, which was to explore the literature on social deviancy. I found the work of researchers who dealt with deviancy as a symbolic system most congenial to my theoretical interests and research findings. Anthropologist Barbara Babcock, in her introduction to *The Reversible World*, stated that scholars interested in symbol often failed to recognize the importance of the negative in cultural communication systems. Historian Natalie Zemon Davis, however, brought the symbolic negative to the forefront in her study of the meanings of the unruly woman as an image in festival and literature of early modern France. Davis's study became a model for my looking at Belle

Gunness, another disorderly woman but this time in twentieth-century America. I approached the figure of the murderess as a symbolic inversion of cultural values.[15]

The third step necessitated my exploring American social history from the turn of the century to the present time, in order to check the working assumption developed above. I did find supportive evidence in the literature. Richard Lingeman's *Small Town America* and Park Dixon Goist's *From Main Street to State Street* were particularly helpful for overviews of American community development, as were Margaret Gibbons Wilson's *The American Woman in Transition: The Urban Influence,* 1870–1920, and William Henry Chafe's *The American Woman: Her Changing Social, Economic, and Political Roles,* 1920–70 for American women's studies. Correspondences emerged in this step that I had not foreseen up to this point. I found that the stories detailing how the mass murderess broke all the rules that operated in an American traditional setting actually touched on the urban transitions which were transforming that culture as well. The Gunness image became a multivalent one, overtly negative in relation to traditional American values but covertly positive in relation to growing urban sensitivities. Social reality coincided with Turner's crisis model.

If one were to ask Martin Barlag, Bob and Ruth Coffeen, Maxine Ford, Dora Rosenow, or Gene McDonald if their stories were sign systems whose referents were attitudes towards modernization, they might, understandably, be taken aback. Yet I hope, once they had looked at these pages, that they would be more than persuaded by my argument but would say, "Why, yes, didn't we tell you that in the first place?"

Clifford Geertz has written in the introduction to his *Interpretation of Cultures* that an ethnographer's task is a hard one. He or she must ask the hard questions, look in the forbidden places to record the inner workings of a culture. All too often, he writes, the field researcher is tempted to escape, to back off. One way to run away for Geertz is "by turning culture into folklore and collecting it" (p. 29). I found quite the opposite to be true in my own field experience. By treating folk art as a semiotic system, an ethnographer can come to an important avenue for interpreting just those cultural patterns which are most inaccessible and which form the bases for our lives and their meaning.

Furthermore, as anthropologist Michael Herzfeld has written, a "semiotic ethnography" has the power to enrich both the study of sign making in general and other research areas through its integrative approach. One aspect of this integration expands the concept of "intertextuality" to truly cross-disciplinary dimensions. To interpret the multiple folk texts constructed of all the overlapping voices speaking about Belle Gunness since the turn of the century, it was necessary to make connections between many disciplinary "texts": anthropology, folkloristics, sociology, history, semiotics, and women's studies, to name the most obvious. Another aspect of this integration stretches the idea of "reflexivity," in which a discipline uses its own methodologies to look back at itself. In this case, accepting storytellers' acts of *bricolage* in constructing a usable metaphor out of the chaos of Belle Gunness's mass murders became a realization that the ethnographer, too, was a *bricoleur* and that all human knowledge was, in fact, built up of worlds "only to be shattered again, and that new worlds were built from the fragments." This recognition of the mosaiclike quality of human thought is the basic theme of Geertz's most recently published essays. He says in the introduction to *Local Knowledge*, "To an ethnographer, sorting through the machinery of distant ideas, the shapes of knowledge are always ineluctably local, indivisible from their instruments and their encasements. One may veil this fact with ecumenical rhetoric or blur it with strenuous theory, but one cannot really make it go away."[16]

Perhaps the Gunness study's validity as a signpost for future research lies in just this embracing local knowledge, integrating and reflecting upon it so that the dichotomy between "folk thought" and "academic analysis" is, if not blurred, made more kaleidoscopic. Bringing the concept of symbolic inversion to bear on a historical event in a small-town American setting, in line with the reflexive movements of anthropologists, breaks the barrier between "self" and "other" in new ways. And crossing and recrossing the boundaries of academic disciplines at different points is an adventure, itself a spur to further inquiry.

Because the historical event of Belle Gunness's murders and oral traditions about that event cannot be clearly distinguished in this case, small-town narrators have constructed various realities from ambiguous evidence. The dichotomy between "reality" and "folklore" and between "reality" and "symbol" is a false one. This study of community narrative points to a reevaluation of those positivist studies which make such a distinction and suggests the symbolic nature of all knowledge. Folk art as symbol becomes a way to construct a reality, not deface it.

APPENDIX

Belle Gunness Ballads

STEWART HOLBROOK, in his 1941 *Murder Out Yonder* (New York: Macmillan Co., 1941), wrote that he heard this ballad sung, most appropriately, to the air of "Love, O Careless Love." Olive Woolley Burt, in her 1958 *American Murder Ballads and Their Stories* (New York: Oxford University Press, 1958), found that none of the ballads is as well known as the stories about the mass murderess, but that this ballad is "the most familiar" (p. 74). The following text is taken from Holbrook, pp. 143–44:

> Belle Gunness lived in In-di-an;
> She always, always had a man;
> Ten at least went in her door—
> And were never, never seen no more.

> Now, all these men were Norska folk
> Who came to Belle from Minn-e-sote;
> They liked their coffee, and their gin:
> They got it—plus a mickey finn.

> And now with cleaver poised so sure
> Belle neatly cut their jug-u-lur [*sic*];
> She put them in a bath of lime,
> And left them there for quite some time.

145

There's red upon the Hoosier moon
For Belle was strong and full of doom;
And think of all them Norska men
Who'll never see St. Paul again.

Burt also presents another ballad text, contributed by Max Egly. This one is the only source for the following verses, to my knowledge (pp. 74–75).

Belle Gunness was a lady fair,
In Indiana State.
She weighed about three hundred pounds,
And that is quite some weight.

That she was stronger than a man
Her neighbors all did own;
She butchered hogs right easily,
And did it all alone.

But hogs were just a side line,
She indulged in now and then;
Her favorite occupation
Was a-butchering of men.

To keep her cleaver busy
Belle would run an ad,
And men would come a-scurrying
With all the cash they had.

Now some say Belle killed only ten,
And some say forty-two;
It was hard to tell exactly,
But there were quite a few.

The bones were dug up in her yard,
Some parts never came to light,
And Belle, herself, could not be found
To set the tally right.

And where Belle is now no one knows,
but my advice is fair:
If a widow advertises
For a man with cash, beware!

"The Ballad of Blood-Thirsty Belle," or "The Ballad of Belle Gunness," composed by Ruth Andrew Coffeen in 1947, is the best-known song about Gunness in LaPorte today. It is sung to the tune of "Pistol-Packin' Mama," but in minor key. The following text is taken from Ruth Coffeen, *Poems: A Small Legacy of Spirit and of Mind* (LaPorte, Indiana: privately printed, 1978):

Belle Gunness was a widow
She and her children three
They came alone
That much is known
To live near our city.

Her husband had insurance
Twas all he had to leave her
So he dropped dead
When on his head
There fell a heavy cleaver.

Lay that cleaver down, Belle,
Lay that cleaver down,
Cleaver-cloutin' Mama
Lay that cleaver down.

She advertised for a husband
And advertising pays
She always knew
Just what to do
For she had such killing ways.

Each suitor who came courtin'
Must first his bride endow
And then that day
Without delay
He fell for her—and how.

Lay that hatchet down, Belle
Lay that hatchet down
Hatchet-hackin' Mama
Lay that hatchet down.

When Andrew Helgelien came,
His check he first cashed in
And then that night
She caught him right
And he was soon bashed in.

Twelve bodies now were buried
Out in her garden row
There may be more,
Some three or four,
No one will ever know.

Lay that shovel down, Belle,
Lay that shovel down,
Shovel-shovin' Mama,
Lay that shovel down.

Things were getting hot for her
To keep up such a race
If you'll permit
We must admit
It was a killing pace.

When Andrew's brother Asa
Had written to inquire
She lost her head
And it is said
She set the place on fire

Lay those matches down, Belle,
Lay those matches down,
Makin'-matches Mama,
Lay those matches down.

The firemen found her bones
And those of her children three
They looked around
But never found
A head for her body.

They couldn't find a head
They couldn't find a skull
So people said
Perhaps instead
She wasn't dead at all.

Lay your head down, Belle
Please lay down your head.
Headless, heartless Mama,
Lay your head down, Belle.

They looked for her in Texas
In sunny Tennessee
They sought her most
From coast to coast
O where, O where was she?

The answer to that question
Is one we now can tell
By [year of performance]
She'll surely be
A-roastin' down in Hell.

The most recent ballad about Belle Gunness was composed and performed by Dallas Turner (".Nevada Slim") of Reno, Nevada in 1976. Nevada Slim is interested in composing ballads on topical events and on murderers in particular. The following version comes from Glenn Ohrlin's rendition at the Ozark Folk Center, Mountain View, Arkansas, on April 8, 1983. Ohrlin's recording of the ballad is available on the Rounder Record label 0158, "The Wild Buckaroo."

Belle Gunness

In old Indiana, not far from LaPorte
There once lived a woman, a home-loving sort.
Belle wanted a husband, she wanted one bad.
She placed in the papers a lonely-hearts ad.

So big, mean and ugly, she stayed to herself.
A sharp cleaver lay on her slaughter-pen shelf.
She was a hog-raiser, she started from scratch
And planted each suitor in her 'tater patch.

Chorus. Young feller, young feller, you love-hungry lad.
You're crazy to answer some lonely-hearts ad.
You might find a true love, you might meet your match.
Or you might be planted in some 'tater patch.

Men wrote to Belle Gunness, she'd rush a reply.
She sent them her picture, the days would slip by.
Then Belle, sweet and loving, would write them and say,
"Come to me, my darling, I know that you'll stay."

Men came to Belle Gunness to share food and bed
Not knowin' that soon they'd be knocked in the head.
But while they were sleepin' she'd lift the door-latch
She'd kill 'em and plant 'em in her 'tater patch.

Chorus

In church every Sunday you'd see pious Belle,
The Devil's own daughter, the Princess of Hell.
Belle Gunness's heaven was her slaughter-pen
For she lived in glory of butchering men.

She wanted their money, she got every cent.
And families was wondering where those fellers went.
Did they meet Belle Gunness, her heart did they catch?
No, each one was planted in Belle's 'tater patch.

Well, early one morning the folks gathered round
Belle Gunness's farmhouse had burned to the ground.
They figured Belle Gunness had been burned to death.
They searched through the embers; they all held their breath.

Could this be Belle Gunness, so mean, so big?
The men didn't think so, they started to dig.
Some thirty-two bodies, her lonely-hearts catch,
Was dug up that morning in Belle's 'tater patch.

Chorus

NOTES

Introduction: *Bricolage*

1. Norris and Ross McWhirter eds., *Guinness Book of World Records*, 1st–12th eds. (New York: Sterling, 1956–74).

2. Belle Gunness has been so called because she, like the ogre Bluebeard in the fairytale, killed multiple spouses (or potential spouses). Willard R. Espy, in his *Thou Improper, Thou Uncommon Noun: An Etymology of Words That Once Were Names* (New York: Clarkson N. Potter, 1978), shows how the term *bluebeard* has generalized to any criminal who kills husbands or wives (p. 165). See chapter 4 for a fuller discussion of this label, which becomes a controlling metaphor for community folk art.

3. Kjell Haarstad, personal communication, 29 March 1976. His information is drawn from local archival records, including an 1865 census report, an 1874 church confirmation record, and 1878 poor-relief rolls, as well as the 1908 *Selbyggen* files. See his *Selbu i fortid og nåtid*, vol. 2, 1837–1945 (Trondheim: 1976), for a fuller community history of Selbu.

4. See Reider Th. Christiansen, ed., *Folktales of Norway*, trans. Pat Shaw Iverson (Chicago: University of Chicago Press, 1964), esp. pp. 79–134.

5. Christiansen, *Folktales*, esp. pp. 147–262; O. E. Rölvaag, *Giants in the Earth* (New York: Harper and Row, 1927); Foss's *Husmandsgutten* is summarized in Ingrid Semmingsen, *Norway to America: A History of the Migration*, trans. Einar Haugen (Minneapolis: University of Minnesota Press, 1978), pp. 138–41; see Semmingsen, *Norway to America*, pp. 121–31, and Theodore C. Blegen, ed. and trans., *Land of Their Choice: The Immigrants Write Home* (Minneapolis: University of Minnesota Press, 1955), for immigrant attitudes towards America.

6. For a generalized history of the shift from earlier family to later single-person migration from Norway, see Theodore C. Blegen's two-

volume study *Norwegian Migration to America*, vol. 1: 1825–1860 (1931), and vol. 2: *American Transition* (1940) (Northfield, Minn.: Norwegian-American Historical Association); Einar Haugen, *The Norwegians in America: A Student's Guide to Localized History* (New York: Teachers' College Press, Columbia University, 1967); Semmingsen, *Norway to America*, pp. 112–13. Information on Belle Gunness's immigration to Chicago is based on Haarstad's analysis of emigrant ships' logs, as well as on Lillian de la Torre, *The Truth about Belle Gunness*, pp. 12–13, and Ann Jones, *Women Who Kill* (New York: Holt, Rinehart and Winston, 1980), pp. 129–30.

7. Jones, *Women Who Kill*, p. 129; Semmingsen, *Norway to America*, p. 129.

8. Generalized information about Belle Gunness's life in LaPorte, Indiana is drawn from de la Torre and Jones. The LaPorte County Historical Society Museum pamphlet *The Gunness Story* is also useful. The museum houses legal documents concerning the Gunness case, including coroners' inquests, a trial summary of *The State of Indiana* v. *Ray Lamphere*, and Belle Gunness's will. The museum has one of Mrs. Gunness's love letters to her last victim, Andrew Helgelien, historical photographs, and a copy of the 1908 romance thriller *The Mrs. Gunness Mystery: A Thrilling Tale of Love, Duplicity, and Crime*, as well as a Gunness exhibit.

Newspaper coverage includes that in the contemporary *LaPorte Argus-Bulletin* and *LaPorte Herald-Chronicle*, as well as the present *LaPorte Herald-Argus*, a result of the two earlier papers' merger in 1924. I thank Martin Barlag for the use of his private newspaper collection. The 1908 *Chicago Tribune*, the *Chicago Record-Herald*, and the *New York Times* were also consulted.

Oral histories and folklore field research reports include the unpublished transcripts of interviews done by Lillian de la Torre, July-August 1952, and the unpublished transcripts of interviews conducted by Indiana University students, 1967–1975, presently housed in the Folklore Institute Archives in Bloomington. My own field research was conducted in 1975–76 and in 1981. Tapes and transcripts are on deposit at the LaPorte County Historical Society Museum. Persons interviewed will be individually footnoted when quoted or referred to in the text.

9. Glenn Ott, interview with author, LaPorte, Indiana, 29 April 1976.

10. Claude Lévi-Strauss, *The Savage Mind*, pp. 16–36; Clifford Geertz, "Religion as a Cultural System," in his *The Interpretation of Cultures*, p. 100.

11. Stewart H. Holbrook, *Murder Out Yonder: An Informal Study of Certain Classic Crimes in Back-Country America* (New York: Macmillan Co., 1941), pp. 240, 143.

12. Richard M. Dorson, "Defining the American Folk Legend," p. 170; Linda Dégh and Andrew Vázsonyi, "Legend and Belief," p. 116.

13. Linda Dégh and Andrew Vázsonyi, "The Dialectics of the Legend."

14. Glenn Ott, interview with author, LaPorte, Indiana, 29 April 1976; Martin Barlag, interview with author, LaPorte, Indiana, 1 June 1976.

15. See Alfred Schutz, *The Problem of Social Reality*, vol. 1 of his *Collected Papers* (The Hague: Martinus Nijhoff, 1967), and Peter Berger and Thomas Luckmann, *The Social Construction of Reality: A Treatise in the*

Sociology of Knowledge (Garden City, N.Y.: Doubleday Anchor, 1967). Roderick J. Roberts, *The Power Boys: The Uses of an Historical Legend,* Monograph Series 9 (Bloomington, Ind: Folklore Publications Group, 1980), shows how Mormon, Anglo, and Chicano versions of a historical event ultimately become vehicles for current tensions between the three groups in southeastern Arizona in a situation analogous to the one presented here.

16. Janet L. Dolgin and JoAnn Magdoff, "The Invisible Event," pp. 351–52.

17. Victor Turner, "Social Dramas and Ritual Metaphors," pp. 23–59, and "Social Dramas and Stories about Them," pp. 141–68; Robert Georges, "The General Concept of Legend: Some Assumptions to Be Reexamined and Reassessed," p. 18; Clifford Geertz, "Thick Description: Toward an Interpretive Theory of Culture," in his *The Interpretation of Cultures,* p. 21. Geertz's comments on the "world in a teacup" model are apropos: "The Jonesville-is-America writ small (or America-is-Jonesville writ large) fallacy is so obviously one that the only thing that needs explanation is how people have managed to believe it and expected others to believe. The notion that one can find the essence of national societies, civilizations, great religions, or whatever summed up and simplified in so-called 'typical' small towns and villages is palpable nonsense" (pp. 21–22). He does go on to say, however, that small facts *do* speak to large issues, because "social actions [here townspeople talking about the mass murderess] are comments on more than themselves" (p. 23).

18. Lillian de la Torre, as quoted in "Lillian de la Torre Bueno McCue," in *Contemporary Authors* (Detroit: Gale Research, 1964); Louise A. Tilly, "Social Sciences and the Study of Women: A Review Article," p. 171; Mary S. Hartman, *Victorian Murderesses,* p. 10.

19. Natalie Zemon Davis, "Women on Top: Symbolic Sexual Inversion and Political Disorder in Early Modern Europe," pp. 147–90; Barbara Babcock defines "symbolic inversion" as "any act of expressive behavior which inverts, contradicts, abrogates, or in some fashion presents an alternative to commonly held cultural codes, values and norms be they linguistic, literary or artistic, religious or social and political" in her introduction to the above volume, p. 14; Park Dixon Goist, *From Main Street to State Street,* pp. 161–64.

20. Geertz, "Thick Description," pp. 10, 28–30; see Robert A. Georges and Michael O. Jones, *People Studying People: The Human Element in Fieldwork* (Berkeley and Los Angeles: University of California Press, 1980), for a discussion of practical, ethical, and theoretical problems involved in field research.

1. "Belle Gunness Put Us on the Map"

1. Historical information on the state of Indiana is drawn from John D. Barnhart and Donald F. Carmony, *Indiana: From Frontier to Industrial Commonwealth,* 2 vols. (New York: Lewis Historical Publishing Co., 1954). Material on the city of LaPorte and LaPorte County is taken from Jasper Packard, *History of LaPorte County, Indiana,* 1876; the Rev. E. D. Daniels, *Twentieth Century History and Biographical Record of LaPorte County,*

Indiana, (Chicago: Lewis Publishing Co., 1904); Edith J. Backus, ed., *LaPorte, Indiana, History of the First Hundred Years, 1832–1932* (LaPorte, Ind.: LaPorte County Historical Society, 1938); *The Portable LaPorte County* (Michigan City, Ind.: Michigan City Public Library and LaPorte County CETA, n.d. but ca. 1980). Archival material at the historical museum and the offices of the *LaPorte Herald-Argus* were also consulted. Demographic statistics are taken from Morton J. Marcus, *Population and Housing Profile: LaPorte County, Indiana,* Census Profile no. 46 (Bloomington, Ind.: Indiana University, Foundation for the School of Business for the Indiana Real Estate Commission, 1973).

2. W. L. Warner, *The Living and the Dead,* pp. 1–100; Robert S. and Helen M. Lynd, *Middletown: A Study in American Culture* (New York: Harcourt, Brace, Jovanivich, 1959).

3. Information is drawn from conversations with Don Benn, associate editor, *LaPorte Herald-Argus,* 1975–76, and from personal observation.

4. LaPorte Chamber of Commerce, *LaPorte, Indiana* (LaPorte: Windsor Publications, 1974), p. 1.

5. *The Portable LaPorte County,* p. 21.

6. Glenn Ott, 29 April 1976; Maxine Ford, 3 April 1976; Louis Blake, 13 September 1975; interviews with author, LaPorte, Indiana.

7. Albert Nicholson, interview with de la Torre, LaPorte, Indiana, July-August 1952.

8. Dora Diesslin Rosenow, interview with author, LaPorte, Indiana, 22 September 1975; Charles Pahrman's analysis of the case influenced de la Torre's *The Truth about Belle Gunness.*

9. Megan Backus, interview with author, Bloomington, Indiana, 20 October 1976.

10. John Nepsha, Jr., interview with author, LaPorte, Indiana, 26 March 1976.

11. De la Torre, *Belle Gunness,* pp. 38–39; Ann Jones, *Women Who Kill,* p. 137; the shed, called "the last known standing relic of the notorious Belle Gunness mystery" in a 10 April 1956 *LaPorte Herald-Argus* article, now stands on LaPorte resident Fred Hoffman's property. It is covered with names, initials, and dates. A neighbor of Mr. Hoffman's, John Diedrich, recalled that visitors, attracted to the Gunness farm, carved on the shed, which was shortly thereafter moved to its present site. As a relic, the building is a visible complement to the narratives which outline the community's notoriety.

12. Gene McDonald, interview with author, LaPorte, Indiana, 10 March 1976; reference to Gunness sale in Gene McDonald, *Lincoln Township Centennial,* (Mill Creek School, Indiana, 1966), p. 33, and in de la Torre, *Belle Gunness,* pp. 50–51.

13. Eldora Hutson Burns, interview with de la Torre, July-August 1952, and with author, 1 March 1976, Michigan City, Indiana.

14. "Gunness Story As Told by Blodgett; Famous Indianapolis News Reporter Covered Crime Here Years Ago; His Tale Never Public," *LaPorte Daily Herald-Argus,* 23 July 1930; de la Torre, *Belle Gunness,* p. 52.

15. Frank J. Kerwin, interview with author, LaPorte, Indiana, 26 January 1976; de la Torre, *Belle Gunness,* esp. pp. 63–159; Lance W. Bennett, "Storytelling in Criminal Trials: A Model of Social Judgement," *Quarterly Journal of Speech* 64, no. 1 (February 1978):1–22.

16. Richard Lingeman, *Small Town America: A Narrative History, 1620–the Present* (Boston: Houghton Mifflin Co., 1980), pp. 321–63.

17. Ruth Andrew Coffeen, interview with author, LaPorte, Indiana, 21 April 1976.

18. Maxine Ray Ford, interview with author, LaPorte, Indiana, 3 April 1976.

19. Indiana University Folklore Institute Archives, IU:3904, Mrs. David Slater, interview with Claudia David, 26 July 1974; Indiana University Folklore Institute Archives, 68/42, Gene McDonald, interview with Janis Mellenthin, LaPorte, Indiana, 31 December 1967.

20. Warner, *Living and the Dead*, pp. 101–226.

21. Robert and Ruth Andrew Coffeen, interview with author, LaPorte, Indiana, 21 April 1976.

22. See Appendix for full ballad text. Text appears under category "Humorous Poems" in Ruth Andrew Coffeen, *Poems: A Small Legacy of Spirit and of Mind* (LaPorte, Ind., 1978); information on the 1947 performance is drawn from Ruth Andrew Coffeen, interview with author, LaPorte, Indiana, 21 April 1976, and the McLane Collection of Women's Literary Society History, LaPorte County Historical Society Museum.

23. Ernst Earnest, *The American Eve in Fact and Fiction, 1775–1914*, pp. 228–29. *The Mrs. Gunness Mystery* showed Belle Gunness, dressed as a Gibson girl, administering poison to a bedridden man on the cover.

24. Information on the 1957 and 1975 performances is drawn from personal communication with Laura Z. Krentz, president, and Forbes Julian, past president, of the Little Theatre Club, and from Maxine Ford, interview with author, 3 April 1976, and Maxine Ford and Juanita Schnable, interview with author, 6 April 1976.

25. Steven James, interview with author, 11 May 1976; Stewart H. Holbrook, *Murder Out Yonder*, p. 240.

26. Information on the "Belle Gunness bust" anecdote drawn from Maxine Ford, interview with author, 3 April 1976, and from W. R. Morrish, publisher of the *LaPorte Herald-Argus*, personal communication, who was one of the transmitters of the story through the service club circuit.

27. Mary Douglas, *Purity and Danger*, pp. 169–70.

2. The Murder Farm

1. Abstract for tract of land, Sec. 26, Town 37 N, range 3 W, filed under John and Catherine Nepsha, Jr., LaPorte Savings and Loan Mortgage, no. 173: Potawatomi Nation to 1826; U.S. Government, 1826–?; Adam G. Polk, ?–1838; John Walker, 1838–46; Harriet Walker Holcomb, 1846–64; William Zahrt, 1864–83; Henry Drebing, 1883–88; Grosvenor H. and Sarah B. Goss, 1888–90; Charles M. Eddy, 1890–92; Mattie Altic, 1892–93; Altic heirs, Emma Applegate and Eva Ruppert, 1893–94; Thomas Boyle, 1894–98; Arthur F. Williams, 1898–1901; Belle Sorensen, 1901.

2. References are apparently to John Walker, Mattie Altic, the Drebings, and the Eddys respectively.

3. Gene McDonald, interview with author, LaPorte, Indiana, 28 August, 1975; 16 September 1975; 31 October 1975; 10 March 1976; 3 April 1976; 17 May 1976; 26 May 1976; 2 June 1976; Indiana University Folklore In-

stitute Archives, 68/42, interview with Janis Mellenthin, 31 December 1967.

4. As quoted by Richard Lingeman, *Small Town America*, p. 356.

5. References are to John Joseph Coughlin and Michael Kenna, two of Chicago's underworld bosses who made the vice districts of the First Ward famous. The Everleigh sisters, Ada and Minna, who kept one of the most elegant houses in Chicago's First Ward, may be models for Gene's discussion of Mattie Altic. See Emmet Dedmon, *Fabulous Chicago* (New York: Random House, 1953), pp. 251–69.

6. Martin Barlag, interviews with author, LaPorte, Indiana, 26 April 1976; 1 June 1976; 13 October 1976.

7. Mark Thomas Connelly, *The Response to Prostitution in the Progressive Era*, pp. 114–35.

8. Ibid., pp. 6–10; See Edgar Morin, *Rumor in Orléans* (London: Anthony Blond, 1971), for a French sociologist's analysis of a rumor about the white-slave traffic that spread through Orléans in May and June of 1969. One of Morin's symbolic interpretations of the meaning of the rumor is that it outlines the political decay of the town center resulting from Orléans's absorption by Paris (p. 71), a thesis comparable to the one developed here.

9. Maxine Ford, interview with author, 23 September 1975; 3 April 1976; 9 April 1976; Charles Cochrane, interview with de la Torre, July-August 1952; Glenn Ott, interview with author, 29 April 1976; Martha Maxson Alderfer, interview with de la Torre, July-August 1952.

10. Liz Smith did, however, give this information when questioned the evening after the fire on 28 April 1908, as reported in her obituary in the *LaPorte Argus-Bulletin*, 18 March 1916. The same article states that she did act as a witness in Lamphere's trial: "Her testimony in the courtroom at his trial was always to shield him." There is no evidence in de la Torre, *Belle Gunness*, that she did so.

11. Almetta Hay, interview with author, LaPorte, Indiana, 26 April 1976; George Heusi, interview with author, LaPorte, Indiana, 10 April 1976; Martha Maxson Alderfer, interview with de la Torre, LaPorte, Indiana, July-August 1952.

12. Maxine Ford, interview with author, LaPorte, Indiana, 3 April 1976; Maxine Ford's parents, the Taylor Rays, were friends of Wirt and Bessie Folant Worden and shared stories about the Gunness case for years afterwards. Mrs. Worden was one of the major contributors to de la Torre's study, so many of the Ray and Ford family narratives parallel discussion in *The Truth about Belle Gunness*.

13. *LaPorte Argus-Bulletin*, 5 May and 8 May 1916.

14. See Mary Douglas, *Natural Symbols;* Marina Warner, in her *Joan of Arc: The Image of Female Heroism* (New York: Knopf, 1981), points out the necessity for fourteenth-century France to perceive Joan of Arc as a virgin, for her body symbolized the body politic invaded on all sides in the wars with the English (pp. 13–31). Here, the bodies and houses of a madam, a town character, and a mass murderess reflect the crumbling of town boundaries, for these women are the community's misfits, not its heroines.

15. See *The Poetry of Robert Frost*, ed. Edward Connery Latham (New York: Holt, Rinehart and Winston, 1969), pp. 33–34.

16. Indiana University Folklore Institute Archives, 68/42, Madeline Kinney and Gene McDonald to interviewer Janis Mellenthin, LaPorte, Indiana, 31 December 1967.

17. Dora Diesslin Rosenow, interview with author, LaPorte, Indiana, 22 September 1975.

18. Albert Nicholson, interview with de la Torre, LaPorte, Indiana, July-August 1952.

19. George Heusi, interview with author, LaPorte, Indiana, 10 April 1976.

20. Dora Diesslin Rosenow, interview with author, LaPorte, Indiana, 22 September 1975.

21. Dora Diesslin Rosenow, interview with author, LaPorte, Indiana, 26 March 1976.

22. Ronald Rosenow, interview with author, LaPorte, Indiana, 26 March, 1976.

23. Albert Nicholson, interview with de la Torre, LaPorte, Indiana, July-August 1952.

24. Dora Diesslin Rosenow, interview with author, LaPorte, Indiana, 22 September 1975.

25. Albert Nicholson, interview with de la Torre, LaPorte, Indiana, July-August 1952.

26. As quoted by Lingeman, *Small Town America*, p. 338.

27. See Arthur J. Vidich and Joseph Bensman, *Small Town in Mass Society*, esp. pp. 319–20.

3. Strong Man or Strong Woman?

1. Lillian de la Torre, *The Truth about Belle Gunness*, p. 167; Louis Blake, interview with author, LaPorte, Indiana, 13 September 1975.

2. As quoted in Clifton Wooldridge, *Twenty Years a Detective in the Wickedest City in the World* . . . . (Chicago: privately printed, 1908), pp. 167–68; see also Cesare Lombroso and William Ferrero, *The Female Offender* (New York: T. F. Unwin, 1895) and "Cesare Lombroso Discusses the Gunness Case," *Chicago Record-Herald*, 3 June 1908.

3. Albert Nicholson, interview with de la Torre, LaPorte, Indiana, July-August 1952.

4. Dora Diesslin Rosenow, interview with author, LaPorte, Indiana, 22 September 1975.

5. Frances Lapham Dawson, interview with de la Torre, LaPorte, Indiana, July-August 1952.

6. Mary Swenson (pseud.), interview with author, LaPorte, Indiana, 6 October 1975.

7. John Mack Faragher, *Women and Men on the Overland Trail*, esp. pp. 122–28.

8. Richard Lingeman, *Small Town America*, p. 311.

9. Barbara Ehrenreich and Deirdre English, *Witches, Midwives, and Nurses: A History of Women Healers*, Glass Mountain Pamphlet, no. 1 (Old Westbury, N.Y.: The Feminist Press, 1973), esp. pp. 33–34, and *Complaints and Disorders: The Sexual Politics of Sickness*, Glass Mountain Pamphlet, no. 2 (Old Westbury, N.Y.: The Feminist Press, 1973), esp. pp. 23–24; Richard W. Wertz and Dorothy C. Wertz, *Lying-in*, esp. pp. 29–108, 128.

10. *The Portable LaPorte County*, (Michigan City, Ind.: Michigan City Public Library and LaPorte County CETA, n.d. but ca. 1980), p. 27.

11. Joanna L. Stratton, *Pioneer Women: Voices from the Kansas Frontier* (New York: Simon and Schuster Touchstone, 1981), p. 87.

12. John Nepsha, Jr., interview with author, LaPorte, Indiana, 25 March 1976; Louis Blake, interview with author, LaPorte, Indiana, 13 September 1975; Gene McDonald, interview with author, LaPorte, Indiana, 10 March 1976; Harold Sabin, "The Belle Gunness Horror Story Still Causes Hoosiers to Quiver" (Stories of State Mark Sesquicentennial Series), *Indianapolis Star*, 24 April 1966.

13. See Stith Thompson, *Motif-Index of Folk Literature* (Bloomington: Indiana University Press, 1957), for strong-man motifs, which include F610 Remarkably strong man, F624 Mighty lifter, F624.1 Strong man lifts horse (ox, ass), X940 Lie: remarkably strong man, and X941 Lie: remarkable lifter. Herbert Halpert's comment in his "Definition and Variation in Folk Legend" in *American Folk Legend* (Berkeley and Los Angeles: University of California Press, 1971), pp. 50–51, that the *Motif-Index* does not have a category for individuals who really are strong, is apropos here.

14. Carol Burke, ed., *Plain Talk* (West Lafayette, Ind.: Purdue University Press, 1983), pp. 88–90; LaPorte County Oral History Cassette Collection, Michigan City Public Library and LaPorte County CETA, T-2-44, Harold L. Welkie, interview with Laurie Radke, Wanatah, Indiana, 17 January 1978.

15. See William Henry Chafe, *The American Woman*, and Margaret Gibbons Wilson, *The American Woman in Transition*.

16. Mabel Carpenter (pseud.), interview with author, LaPorte, Indiana, 12 April 1976.

17. Lucia Egle, interview with author, Michigan City, Indiana, 9 March 1976.

18. Blanche Payne, *History of Costume: From the Ancient Egyptians to the Twentieth Century* (New York: Harper and Row, 1965), pp. 530–32. Payne writes that a "characteristic gesture of an 1890 belle was to fluff out her [leg-of-mutton] sleeves upon removing her wrap" (p. 531).

19. Indiana University Folklore Institute Archives, Legend file IU:2188, Winnie Nillson, interview with Paula Richmond, 16 November 1972; 71:459, Diane Mitzner, interview with Nancy Schaffer, 16 September 1971; 70:22, Debora Keller, interview with Wanda Lou Hunt, 24 September 1969.

20. Indiana University Folklore Institute Archives, Legend file IU:2390–93, Barbara Howes, collector; IU:2940, Mendy Pugh, interview with Mark Leffers, 19 October 1970.

21. Lois W. Banner, *American Beauty*.

22. Indiana University Folklore Institute Archives, IU:2893, Mrs. Howard McLane, interview with Barbara Howes, LaPorte, Indiana, 1972; Dorothy Rowley, interview with author, LaPorte, Indiana, 5 September 1975.

23. Mary Swenson (pseud.), interview with author, 6 October 1975.

24. Eldora Hutson Burns, interview with author, Michigan City, Indiana, 1 March 1976, and with de la Torre, July-August 1952; Robert and Ruth Andrew Coffeen, interview with author, LaPorte, Indiana, 21 April 1976.

25. Gene McDonald, interview with author, LaPorte, Indiana, 10 March 1976.

26. Stith Thompson, *The Folktale*, labels this tale, Type 425A in his type index, as "The Monster (Animal) Bridegroom," pp. 98–100; James Fernandez, "The Mission of Metaphor in Expressive Culture," pp. 120–23, and Edmund Leach, "Anthropological Aspects of Language: Animal Categories and Verbal Abuse," pp. 23–63, discuss the metaphorical use of animals in labeling deviant humans. Historian Carroll Smith-Rosenberg, personal communication, noted that women were often called by animal names in the nineteenth century. I'm suggesting here that Belle's fur coat is semiotically charged with similar meanings.

27. Orrin Klapp, "American Villain Types," pp. 337–40.

28. Orrin Klapp, *Heroes, Villains, and Fools*, pp. 58–59.

4. The Lady Bluebeard

1. Indiana University Folklore Institute Archives, Legend file IU:2188, Winnie Nillson, interview with Paula Richmond, 16 November 1972.

2. Stith Thompson, *The Folktale*, pp. 36, 173. Thompson places these two types (Type 311 and Type 312 in his system of noting folktale plots) under the broad category of "Ogres and Witches."

3. Lucia Egle, interview with author, Michigan City, Indiana, 9 March 1976.

4. Carrie Garwood Davis, interview with author, LaPorte, Indiana, 17 October 1975.

5. George Heusi, interview with author, LaPorte, Indiana, 25 March 1976.

6. LaPorte County Historical Society Museum, Inquest of Belle Gunness, Deposition of Witness Frank K. Coffeen, 12 May 1908.

7. Frank K. Coffeen interview with de la Torre, LaPorte, Indiana, July-August 1952.

8. Robert Coffeen, interview with author, LaPorte, Indiana, 21 April 1976.

9. Lillian de la Torre, *The Truth about Belle Gunness*, p. 40, writes, "There was a good deal of gabble about her conducting a baby farm where she freely abolished her little charges. The only actual evidence that Mrs. Gunness boarded children as well as adopting them, however, was offered by a nursling who survived." The tradition of Belle's murdering babies also appears in Henry K. Vernon, "Belle Gunness: 'The Female Bluebeard,'" in a nondated crime detective pamphlet entitled *Crimes of Love and Passion*, no. 2, ca. 1920, p. 21.

10. Frances Lapham Dawson, interview with de la Torre, LaPorte, Indiana, July-August 1952; Eldora Hutson Burns, interview with author, Michigan City, Indiana, 1 March 1976.

11. Francis Lapham Dawson, interview with de la Torre, LaPorte, Indiana, July–August, 1952; Indiana University Folklore Institute Archives, IU:3901, Joyce M. Cook, interview with Claudia David, 28 July 1974; Ann Jones, *Women Who Kill*, p. 355, n. for p. 130.

12. LaPorte County Historical Society Museum, Inquest of Jennie Olsen, Deposition of Witness, 12 May 1908.

13. Vernon, "Belle Gunness," pp. 24–31.

14. Gene McDonald, interview with author, LaPorte, Indiana, 10 March 1976.

15. Martha Maxson Alderfer, interview with de la Torre, LaPorte, Indiana, July-August 1952.

16. See Appendix for full ballad text, which appeared originally in Olive Woolley Burt, *American Murder Ballads and Their Stories* (New York: Oxford University Press, 1958), pp. 74–75; Almetta Hay, interview with author, LaPorte, Indiana, 26 April 1976; Emmett Dedmon, *Fabulous Chicago* (New York: Random House, 1953), pp. 136–37, writes, "One of the saloon proprietors of the day was an ex-pickpocket who owned the Lone Star saloon and Palm Garden at the southern end of Whiskey Row. His name was Mickey Finn. Among the drinks he offered to his [Chicago] patrons were a 'Mickey Finn Special' and a 'Number Two.' The Mickey Finn Special was compounded of raw alcohol, water in which snuff had been soaked and a mysterious white ingredient Finn had obtained from a voodoo doctor . . . . A Mickey Finn Special could render a victim unconscious for two or three days, enabling the ingenious Finn to stack up his dupes in the back room without missing a turn at the bar where other customers might be clamoring for one of the *specialités de la maison*. At his leisure Finn would rifle the pockets of the doped patrons and dump them into the street."

17. See Appendix for full ballad texts.

18. Indiana University Folklore Institute Archives, 70:22, Debora Keller, interview with Wanda Lou Hunt, 24 September 1969; 70:115, Bob Fischer, interview with Carol David, 24 February 1969.

19. LaPorte County Historical Society Museum, Andrew Helgelien Inquest, Deposition of Witness Asle K. Helgelien, 5 May 1908.

20. Glenn Ott, interview with author, LaPorte, Indiana, 29 April 1976.

21. Modern belief tales include "The Hook," in which a parking couple is threatened by an insane man with a hook for an arm; "The Boyfriend's Death," in which a girl finds her boyfriend mutilated and hanging above their parked car; "The Roommate's Death," in which a college roommate finds her girlfriend outside their dormitory room with a hatchet in her back or head; and "The Man in the Back Seat," in which a lone woman driver is saved by a truck driver from a man in the back seat with a hatchet.

22. Elaine Tyler May, *Great Expectations.*

23. Mary S. Hartman, *Victorian Murderesses*, passim; Jones, *Women Who Kill*, esp. pp. 63–77; May, *Great Expectations*, esp. pp. 75–163.

24. Dora Diesslin Rosenow, interview with author, LaPorte, Indiana, 22 September 1975.

25. Henry Johnson, interview with author, New Carlisle, Indiana, 3 May 1976.

26. See Michelle Zimbalist Rosaldo, "Woman, Culture, and Society: A Theoretical Overview," pp. 17–42, and her "The Use and Abuse of Anthropology: Reflections on Feminism and Cross-Cultural Understanding," and Jane Monnig Atkinson, "Anthropology," *Signs: Journal of Women in Culture and Society* 8, no. 2 (Winter 1982):236–58, for a discussion of cultural sexual asymmetry. See J. L. Fischer, "The Sociopsychological Analysis of Folktales," for a discussion of the relationship of traditional fantasy (myths and folktales) to cultural realities.

27. LaPorte County Historical Society Museum, Andrew Helgelien Inquest, Deposition of Asle K. Helgelien, 5 May 1908. De la Torre, personal communication, pointed out the moving passage in the deposition.

28. As the court transcripts for the Lamphere trial are now missing, I am depending on these sources: the November 1908 coverage in the *LaPorte Argus-Bulletin* and de la Torre, pp. 94–100. A 17 November 1908 *Argus-Bulletin* headline reads: "State Offers Three of the Epistles [Belle Gunness's love letters to Andrew Helgelien] as Evidence Following the Dramatic Narrative of Asle Helgelien—State Makes Progress."

29. Henry Johnson, interview with author, New Carlisle, Indiana, 3 May 1976. See John Mack Faragher, *Women and Men on the Overland Trail*, pp. 132–33, for application of Basil Bernstein's restricted linguistic code to Midwestern male speech and diary writing.

30. Maxine Ray Ford, interview with author, LaPorte, Indiana, 3 April 1976. See Faragher, *Overland Trail*, pp. 132–33, for application of Bernstein's elaborated linguistic code to Midwestern female speech and diary writing.

31. Data come from the ongoing American Kinship Project, University of Chicago, Department of Anthropology. Publications include David M. Schneider, *American Kinship*; David M. Schneider and Calvert B. Cottrell, *The American Kin Universe: A Genealogical Study*, University of Chicago Series in Anthropology: Social, Cultural, Linguistic Anthropology Series, no. 3 (Chicago: University of Chicago, Department of Anthropology, 1975); David M. Schneider and Raymond T. Smith, *Class Differences and Sex Roles in American Kinship and Family Structure* (Englewood Cliffs, N.J.: Prentice-Hall, 1973).

32. Richard Jensen, "Midwestern Transformation: From Traditional Pioneers to Modern Society," pp. 6–11.

33. Donald Woodford, grandson of Asle Helgelien, personal communication, 15 December 1976, and LaPorte County Historical Society Museum correspondence, 1973, said that his grandfather died about 1912 in South Dakota. There was a severe hail storm, and he was out trying to find his son Newton. Newton was safe under a wagon, but Asle was injured and died about a year later from complications. His family remembered him as one who was very concerned about the welfare of his "blood" family, as evidenced by his search for his brother Andrew and for his son.

5. Coining Cupid's Wiles

1. LaPorte County Historical Society Museum, Inquest of Peter Gunness, Depositions of Witnesses Belle Gunness, Swan Nicholson, and Jennie Olsen, 18 December 1902.

2. Mrs. Swan and Albert Nicholson, interview with de la Torre, LaPorte, Indiana, July-August 1952.

3. Ruth Andrew Coffeen, interview with author, LaPorte, Indiana, 21 April 1976.

4. Dr. Poe's play is in manuscript form; it was first written in 1963, while he was a professor of speech at the University of Southwestern Louisiana in Lafayette, and was later revised in 1965 and 1972. Playwright James Forsyth has said that "the characters supporting the central character are as clear cut as a Midwest primitive painting, and rather deeper in definition."

5. As quoted in de la Torre, *The Truth about Belle Gunness*, p. 53.

6. Gene McDonald and Ruth Tallant, conversation recorded by author, LaPorte, Indiana, 10 March 1976.

7. George Heusi, interview with author, LaPorte, Indiana, 25 March 1976.

8. See Appendix for full ballad text.

9. Fred Hoffman, interview with author, LaPorte, Indiana, 8 April 1976; Indiana University Folklore Institute Archives, 68/42, Randy Hopkins, interview with Janis Mellenthin, 31 December 1967.

10. Indiana University Folklore Institute Archives, Legend file IU:3903, Raymond Cox, Jr., interview with Donna Terry, 26 July 1974; Jerry Snyder, interview with author, LaPorte, Indiana 6 May 1976.

11. Maxine Ray Ford, interview with author, LaPorte, Indiana, 3 April 1976. Foreign matter in food—worms, spider eggs, mice, rats, and rodent hair—is the subject of many modern belief legends and rumors.

12. Martin Barlag, interview with author, LaPorte, Indiana, 26 April 1976.

13. Jake and Susie Jones (pseud.), conversation recorded by author, LaPorte, Indiana, 19 May 1976.

14. Edmund R. Leach, "Anthropological Aspects of Language: Animal Categories and Verbal Abuse," pp. 23–63.

15. Richard M. Dorson, in *American Folklore*, pp. 98–99, discusses Ozark variations of the tale and the provenance of the song. Roger E. Mitchell, in his article "The Press, Rumor, and Legend Formation," p. 9, discusses legends about real-life murderer Ed Gein of Plainfield, Wisconsin, in which the farmer is said, incorrectly, to be a cannibal and to keep sweet sausage made out of his women victims in his freezer.

16. Ann Jones, *Women Who Kill*, pp. 137–38; John Mack Faragher, *Women and Men on the Overland Trail*, p. 242, nn. 58–61.
Overland Trail, p. 242, nn. 58–61.

17. See Claude Lévi-Strauss, *The Elementary Structures of Kinship* (Paris, 1949; London: Eyre and Spottiswoode, 1969), for elaboration of this thesis cross-culturally.

18. Faragher, *Overland Trail*, pp. 110–78.

19. Jones, *Women Who Kill*, pp. 138–39; Clifton Wooldridge, *Twenty Years a Detective in the Wickedest City in the World . . .* (Chicago: Privately printed, 1908), pp. 119–91.

20. Elaine Tyler May, *Great Expectations*, pp. 137–56.

21. William Lloyd Warner, *The Living and the Dead*, pp. 160–215.

22. Gretchen Tyler, interview with author, LaPorte, Indiana, 17 May 1976.

6. Belle Gunness Is Alive and Well

1. Forbes Julian, interview with author, LaPorte, Indiana, 26 November 1975; Bob Coffeen, interview with author, LaPorte, Indiana, 21 April 1976; George Heusi, interview with author, 25 March 1976.

2. Mary Swenson (pseud.), interview with author, LaPorte, Indiana, 6 October 1975.

3. Glenn Ott, interview with author, LaPorte, Indiana, 29 April 1976.

4. LaPorte County Historical Society Museum, Belle Gunness Inquest.

5. LaPorte County Courthouse, Complete Court Records, book X, 1885–1909, September Term, 1908, S. 1061. *The State of Indiana* v. *Ray Lamphere*, pp. 433–48. The best coverage is in de la Torre, *The Truth about Belle Gunness*.

6. Eldora Hutson Burns, interview with de la Torre, LaPorte, Indiana, July-August 1952, and interview with author, Michigan City, Indiana, 1 March 1976.

7. John Nepsha, Jr., interview with author, LaPorte, Indiana, 25 March 1976.

8. Donald Woodford, personal communication, Gettysburg, South Dakota, 1973–76.

9. Indiana University Folklore Institute Archives, Miriam Terry.

10. Gene McDonald, Art Flickinger, Evelyn Nordyke, conversation recorded by author, LaPorte, Indiana, 17 October 1976.

11. Lillian de la Torre, *The Coffee Cup*, pp. 60–81.

12. Louis Blake, interview with author, LaPorte, Indiana, 13 September 1975.

13. See Barbara Babcock-Abrahams, "'A Tolerated Margin of Mess': The Trickster and His Tales Reconsidered," pp. 147–86; Richard M. Dorson, *American Folklore*, passim; Paul Radin, *The Trickster: A Study in American Indian Mythology* (New York: Philosophical Library, 1956); Stith Thompson, "The Trickster Cycle," in his *The Folktale*, pp. 319–28; and Barre Toelken, "Ma'i Joldloshi," in *American Folk Legend: A Symposium*, ed. Wayland D. Hand (Berkeley and Los Angeles: University of California Press, 1971), pp. 203–11.

14. Philip Nusbaum, personal communication, 1976.

15. See Appendix for full ballad text.

16. Stewart Holbrook, "Belle, the Female Bluebeard," pp. 218–26; Correspondence between Holbrook and John Black (pseud.), 1941, Stewart Holbrook papers, Manuscripts Section, University of Washington Libraries.

17. Alfred Fox (pseud.), interview with author, 12 May 1976.

18. Homer Croy, *Jesse James Was My Neighbor* (New York: Duell, Sloan and Pearce, 1949), pp. 247ff.; Charles Leland Sonnichsen and William V. Morrison, *Alias Billy the Kid* (Albuquerque: University of New Mexico Press, 1955).

19. Roger Abrahams, "Some Varieties of Heroes in America," pp. 341–62.

20. Indiana University Folklore Institute Archives, 70/17, Ramona Hernandez, collector, 24 September 1969.

21. Gerri Wallis, interview with author, LaPorte, Indiana, 7 May 1976; Lloyd Lewis, *Myths after Lincoln* (New York: Harcourt, Brace, 1929, reprinted 1940), pp. 299ff; Bruce A. Rosenberg, "Custer and the Epic of Defeat," *Journal of American Folklore* 88: 165–77.

22. See Jan Brunvand, *The Vanishing Hitchhiker: American Urban Legends and Their Meanings* (New York: W. W. Norton and Co., 1981) and *The Choking Doberman and Other "New" American Urban Legends* (New York: W. W. Norton and Co., 1984).

Conclusion: *Bricolage* Reconsidered

1. Stewart Holbrook, *Murder Out Yonder* (New York: Macmillan Co., 1941), p. 143.

2. Gordon W. Allport and Leo Postman, *The Psychology of Rumor* (New York: H. Holt and Co., 1947), pp. 75, 100; Gyula Ortutay, "Principles of Oral Transmission," *Acta Ethnographica* (1959): 175–221.

3. Ortutay, "Principles," pp. 175–221; Warren A. Peterson and Noel P. Gist, "Rumor and Public Opinion," *American Journal of Sociology* 57 (September 1951): 159–67.

4. Ortutay, "Principles," pp. 175–221; J. L. Fischer, "The Sociopsychological Analysis of Folktales," p. 242.

5. Information for the Bender family narratives taken from William E. Koch and Mary Frances White, "Legends," in *Kansas Folklore*, ed. by S. J. Sackett and William E. Koch (Lincoln: University of Nebraska Press, 1961), pp. 62–69, and Robert F. Scott, "What Happened to the Benders?" *Western Folklore* 9:4 (1950): 327–37.

6. Roger E. Mitchell, "The Press, Rumor, and Legend Formation," pp. 9, 11.

7. See Vincent Bugliosi, *Helter Skelter: the True Story of the Manson Murders* (New York: Norton, 1974), and Ed Sanders, *The Family: The Story of Charles Manson's Dune Buggy Attack Battalion* (New York: Dutton, 1971).

8. See J. O. Kesselring, "Arsenic and Old Lace," in *The Best Plays of 1940–41*, ed. by Burns Mantle (New York: Dodd, Mead and Co., 1941).

9. Allport and Postman, *Psychology of Rumor*, pp. 75, 100.

10. Richard M. Dorson, "Local History and Folklore," pp. 146–47; Robert Darnton, "Peasants Tell Tales: The Meaning of Mother Goose" and "Workers Revolt: The Great Cat Massacre of the Rue Saint-Severin," in his *The Great Cat Massacre and Other Episodes in French Cultural History* (New York: Basic Books, 1984), pp. 9–106, and John Mack Faragher, *Women and Men on the Overland Trail*.

11. Victor Turner, "Social Dramas and Ritual Metaphors," pp. 23–59.

12. Ibid.

13. Ibid.

14. Lillian de la Torre, *The Coffee Cup*, pp. 60–81.

15. Barbara Babcock, introduction to *The Reversible World*, pp. 13–15, and Natalie Zemon Davis, "Women on Top: Symbolic Sexual Inversion and Political Disorder in Early Modern Europe," pp. 147–90.

16. Michael Herzfeld, "Signs in the Field: Prospects and Issues for Semiotic Ethnography," pp. 99–103; see also *A Crack in the Mirror: Reflexive Perspectives in Anthropology*, ed. by Jay Ruby (Philadelphia: University of Pennsylvania Press, 1982); Franz Boas, as quoted by Claude Lévi-Strauss, "The Structural Study of Myth," in *Myth: A Symposium*, ed. by Thomas A. Sebeok (Bloomington: Indiana University Press, 1971, ca. 1955), p. 81; Clifford Geertz, *Local Knowledge*, p. 4.

SELECT BIBLIOGRAPHY

1. Interviews

Alderfer, Isaiah. Interview with Lillian de la Torre. LaPorte, Indiana, July-August 1952.

Alderfer, Martha Maxson. Interview with Lillian de la Torre. LaPorte, Indiana, July-August 1952.

Backus, Megàn. Interview with author. Bloomington, Indiana, 20 October 1976.

Barlag, Martin. Interviews with author. LaPorte, Indiana, 26 April, 1 June, and 13 October 1976.

Blake, Louis. Interview with author. LaPorte, Indiana, 13 September 1975.

Burns, Eldora Hutson. Interview with Lillian de la Torre. LaPorte, Indiana, July-August 1952. Interview with author. Michigan City, Indiana, 1 March 1976.

Carpenter, Mabel [pseud.]. Interview with author. LaPorte, Indiana, 12 April 1976.

Cochrane, Charles. Interview with Lillian de la Torre. LaPorte, Indiana, July-August 1952.

Coffeen, Frank K. Interview with Lillian de la Torre. LaPorte, Indiana, July-August 1952.

Coffeen, Robert J. Interview with author. LaPorte, Indiana, 21 April 1976.

Coffeen, Ruth Andrew. Interview with author. LaPorte, Indiana, 21 April 1976.

Cook, Joyce M. Interview with Claudia David. LaPorte, Indiana, 28 July 1974. Indiana University Folklore Institute Archives: 3901.

Cox, Raymond Jr. Interview with Donna Terry. LaPorte, Indiana, 26 July 1974. Indiana University Folklore Institute Archives: 3903.

Davis, Carrie Garwood. Interview with author. LaPorte, Indiana, 17 October 1975.

Dawson, Frances Lapham. Interview with Lillian de la Torre. LaPorte, Indiana, July-August 1952.

Egle, Lucia Racher. Interview with author. Michigan City, Indiana, 9 March 1976.

Fischer, Bob. Interview with Carol David. LaPorte, Indiana, 24 February 1969. Indiana University Folklore Institute Archives: Legend file 70:115.

Flickinger, Art. Conversation recorded by author. LaPorte, Indiana, 17 October 1976.

Ford, Maxine Ray. Interviews with author. LaPorte, Indiana, 23 September 1975; 3 April, 6 April, and 9 April 1976.

Fox, Alfred [pseud.]. Interview with author. LaPorte, Indiana, 12 May 1976.

Hay, Almetta. Interview with author. LaPorte, Indiana, 26 April 1976.

Heusi, George. Interview with author. LaPorte, Indiana, 10 April 1976.

Hoffman, Fred. Interview with author. LaPorte, Indiana, 8 April 1976.

Hopkins, Randy. Interview with Janis Mellenthin. LaPorte, Indiana, 31 December 1967. Indiana University Folklore Institute Archives: 68/42.

James, Steve. Interview with author. LaPorte, Indiana, 11 May 1976.

Johnson, Henry. Interview with author. New Carlisle, Indiana, 3 May 1976.

Jones, Jake [pseud.]. Interview with author. LaPorte, Indiana, 19 May 1976.

Jones, Susan [pseud.]. Interview with author. LaPorte, Indiana, 19 May 1976.

Julian, Forbes. Interview with author. LaPorte, Indiana, 26 November 1975.

Keller, Debora. Interview with Wanda Lou Hunt. LaPorte, Indiana, 24 September 1969. Indiana University Folklore Institute Archives: Legend file 70:22.

Kerwin, Frank. Interview with author. LaPorte, Indiana, 26 January 1976.

Kinney, Madeleine. Interview with Janis Mellenthin. LaPorte, Indiana, 31 December 1967. Indiana University Folklore Institute Archives: 68/42.

McDonald, Eugene. Interview with Janis Mellenthin. LaPorte, Indiana, 31 December 1967. Indiana University Folklore Institute Archives: 68/42. Interviews with the author. LaPorte, Indiana, 28 August, 16 September, and 31 October 1975; 10 March, 3 April, 17 May, 26 May, and 2 June 1976.

McLane, Mrs. Howard. Interview with Barbara Howes. LaPorte, Indiana, 16 March 1972. Indiana University Folklore Institute Archives: 2890-2893.

Mitzner, Diane. Interview with Nancy Schaffer. LaPorte, Indiana, 16 September 1971. Indiana University Folklore Institute Archives: Legend file 71:459.

Nepsha, John Jr. Interview with author. LaPorte, Indiana, 26 March 1976.

Nicholson, Albert. Interview with Lillian de la Torre. LaPorte, Indiana, July-August 1952.

Nicholson, Mrs. Swan. Interview with Lillian de la Torre. LaPorte, Indiana, July-August 1952.

Nillson, Winnie. Interview with, Paula Richmond. LaPorte, Indiana, 16 November 1972. Indiana University Folklore Institute Archives: 2188.

Nordyke, Evelyn. Conversation recorded by author. LaPorte, Indiana, 17 October 1976.

Ott, Glenn. Interview with author. LaPorte, Indiana, 29 April 1976.

Pahrman, Charles. Interview with Lillian de la Torre. LaPorte, Indiana, July-August 1952.

Pugh, Mendy. Interview with Mark Leffers. Bloomington, Indiana, 19 October 1970. Indiana University Folklore Institute Archives: 2940.

Rosenow, Dora Diesslin. Interviews with author. LaPorte, Indiana, 22 September 1975 and 26 March 1976.

Rosenow, Ronald. Interview with author. LaPorte, Indiana, 26 March 1976.

Rowley, Dorothy. Interview with author. LaPorte, Indiana, 5 September 1975.

Schnable, Juanita. Interview with author. LaPorte, Indiana, 6 April 1976.

Slater, Mrs. David. Interview with Claudia David. LaPorte, Indiana, 26 July 1974. Indiana University Folklore Institute Archives: 3904.

Snyder, Jerry. Interview with author. LaPorte, Indiana, 6 May 1976.

Swenson, Mary [pseud.]. Interview with author. LaPorte, Indiana, 26 October 1975.

Tallant, Ruth. Conversation recorded by author. LaPorte, Indiana, 10 March 1976.

Tyler. Gretchen. Interview with author. LaPorte, Indiana, 17 May 1976.

Wallis, Gerri. Interview with author. LaPorte, Indiana, 7 May 1976.

Welkie, Harold L. Interview with Laurie Radke, Wanatah, Indiana, 17 January 1978. LaPorte County Oral History Cassette Collection, Michigan City Public Library and LaPorte County CETA, T-2-44.

2. Works Concerning Belle Gunness

Burt, Olive Woolley. "The Profit Motive." In her *American Murder Ballads and Their Stories*. New York: Oxford University Press, 1958.

Coffeen, Ruth Andrew. "The Ballad of Belle Gunness." In *Poems: A Small Legacy of Spirit and of Mind*. LaPorte, Ind.: Privately printed, 1978.

De la Torre, Lillian. "The Coffee Cup." In *Butcher, Baker, Murder Maker: Stories by Members of the Mystery Writers of America*. New York: Borzoi Books, 1954.

———. *The Truth about Belle Gunness*. New York: Fawcett, 1955.

The Gunness Story. LaPorte, Ind.: LaPorte County Historical Society, n.d.

Holbrook, Stewart. "Belle, the Female Bluebeard." *American Mercury* 53, no. 212 (August 1941): 218–26.

———. "Belle of Indiana." In his *Murder Out Yonder: An Informal Study of Certain Classic Crimes in Back-Country America*. New York: Macmillan Co., 1941.

Jones, Ann. "Domestic Atrocity." In her *Women Who Kill*. New York: Holt, Rinehart and Winston, 1980.

Langlois, Janet L. "Belle Gunness, the Lady Bluebeard: Community

Legend as Metaphor." *Journal of the Folklore Institute* 15, no. 2 (May–
August 1978): 147–60.

————. "Belle Gunness, the Lady Bluebeard: Symbolic Inversion in Verbal
Art and American Culture." *Signs: Journal of Women in Culture and
Society* 8, no. 4 (Summer 1983): 617–34.

————. "Belle Gunness, the Lady Bluebeard: Narrative Use of a Deviant
Woman." In *Women's Folklore/Women's Culture*, edited by Rosan Jordan
and Susan Kalcik, Publications of the American Folklore Society, New
Series. Philadelphia: University of Pennsylvania, 1985.

The Mrs. Gunness Mystery: A Thrilling Tale of Love, Duplicity, and Crime.
Chicago: Thompson and Thomas, 1908.

Poe, Harold W. "*Gnista:* A Play in Three Acts." Unpublished script, 1963.

Wooldridge, Clifton. "The Horrible Gunness Farm." In "Coining Cupid's
Wiles," chapter in his *Twenty Years a Detective in the Wickedest City in
the World* . . . . Chicago: Privately printed, 1908.

3.   Theoretical and Historical Works Consulted

Abrahams, Roger. "Some Varieties of Heroes in America." *Journal of the
Folklore Institute* 3, no. 3 (1966):341–62.

Babcock, Barbara. Introduction to *The Reversible World: Symbolic Inversion in Art and Society*, edited by Barbara Babcock. Symbol, Myth, and
Ritual Series. Ithaca, N.Y.: Cornell University Press, 1978.

Babcock-Abrahams, Barbara. "'A Tolerated Margin of Mess': The Trickster and His Tales Reconsidered." *Journal of the Folklore Institute* 11,
no. 3 (1974–75):147–86.

Banner, Lois W. *American Beauty: A Social History . . . through Two Centuries . . . of the American Idea, Ideal, and Image of the Beautiful Woman.* New York: Alfred A. Knopf, 1983.

Chafe, William Henry. *The American Woman: Her Changing Social, Economic, and Political Roles, 1920–1970.* New York: Oxford University
Press, 1972.

Connelly, Mark Thomas. *The Response to Prostitution in the Progressive
Era.* Chapel Hill: University of North Carolina Press, 1980.

Davis, Natalie Zemon. "Women on Top: Symbolic Sexual Inversion and
Political Disorder in Early Modern Europe." In *The Reversible World*,
edited by Barbara Babcock. Ithaca, N.Y.: Cornell University Press,
1978.

Dégh, Linda, and Vázsonyi, Andrew. "The Dialectics of the Legend."
Folklore Preprint Series 1:6. Bloomington, Ind.: Folklore Publications
Group, 1973.

————. "Legend and Belief." In *Folklore Genres*, edited by Dan Ben-Amos.
Publications of the American Folklore Society, vol. 26. Austin: University of Texas Press, 1976.

Dolgin, Janet L., and Magdoff, JoAnn. "The Invisible Event." In *Symbolic
Anthropology: A Reader in the Study of Symbols and Meanings*, edited
by Janet L. Dolgin, David S. Kemnitzer, and David M. Schneider. New
York: Columbia University Press, 1977.

Dorson, Richard M. *American Folklore.* The Chicago History of American
Civilization. Chicago: University of Chicago Press, 1959.

————. "Defining the American Folk Legend." In his *American Folklore and the Historian*. Chicago: University of Chicago Press, 1971.

————. "Local History and Folklore." In his *American Folklore and the Historian*. Chicago: University of Chicago Press, 1971.

Douglas Mary. *Natural Symbols: Explorations in Cosmology*. New York: Random House, 1970, 1973.

————. *Purity and Danger: An Analysis of the Concepts of Pollution and Taboo*. London: Routledge and Kegan Paul, 1966.

Earnest, Ernst. *The American Eve in Fact and Fiction, 1775–1914*. Urbana: University of Illinois Press, 1974.

Faragher, John Mack. *Women and Men on the Overland Trail*. Yale Historical Publications, Miscellany, no. 121. New Haven: Yale University Press, 1979.

Fernandez, James. "The Mission of Metaphor in Expressive Culture." *Current Anthropology* 15, no. 2 (1974):119–45.

Fischer, J. L. "The Sociopsychological Analysis of Folktales." *Current Anthropology* 4, no. 3 (1963):235–72.

Geertz, Clifford. *The Interpretation of Cultures*. New York: Basic Books, 1973.

————. *Local Knowledge: Further Essays in Interpretive Anthropology*. New York: Basic Books, 1983.

Georges, Robert. "The General Concept of Legend: Some Assumptions to Be Reexamined and Reassessed." In *American Folk Legend: A Symposium*, edited by Wayland D. Hand. Berkeley and Los Angeles: University of California Press, 1971.

Goist, Park Dixon. *From Main Street to State Street: Town, City, and Community in America*. Interdisciplinary Urban Series. Port Washington, N.Y.: National University Publications, Kennikat Press, 1977.

Hartman, Mary S. *Victorian Murderesses: A True History of Thirteen Respectable French and English Women Accused of Unspeakable Crimes*. New York: Schocken Books, 1977.

Herzfeld, Michael. "Signs in the Field: Prospects and Issues for Semiotic Ethnography." *Semiotica* (special issue *Signs in the Field: Semiotic Perspectives on Ethnography*) 46, no. 2/4 (1983): 99–103.

Jensen, Richard. "Midwestern Transformation: From Traditional Pioneers to Modern Society." In *Local History Today: Papers Presented at Four Regional Workshops for Local History Organizations in Indiana, June, 1978 to April, 1979*. Indianapolis: Indiana Historical Society, 1979.

Klapp, Orrin. "American Villain Types." *American Sociological Review* 21 (1956): 337–40.

————. *Heroes, Villains, and Fools: The Changing American Character*. Englewood Cliffs, N.J.: Prentice-Hall, 1968.

Leach, Edmund. "Anthropological Aspects of Language: Animal Categories and Verbal Abuse." In *New Directions in the Study of Language*, edited by E. H. Lenneberg. Cambridge: MIT Press, 1965.

Lévi-Strauss, Claude. *The Savage Mind*. Chicago: University of Chicago Press, 1966. (English translation of *La pensée sauvage*. Paris: Plon, 1962.)

Lingeman, Richard. *Small Town America: A Narrative History, 1620–the Present*. Boston: Houghton Mifflin Co., 1980.

May, Elaine Tyler. *Great Expectations: Marriage and Divorce in Post-Victorian America*. Chicago: University of Chicago Press, 1980.

Mitchell, Roger E. "The Press, Rumor, and Legend Formation." *Midwestern Journal of Language and Folklore* 5, no. 1.2 (Spring/Fall 1979): 5–61.

Rosaldo, Michelle Zimbalist. "Woman, Culture, and Society: A Theoretical Overview." In *Woman, Culture, and Society*, edited by Michelle Zimbalist Rosaldo and Louise Lamphere. Stanford, Calif.: Stanford University Press, 1974.

————. "The Use and Abuse of Anthropology: Reflections on Feminism and Cross-cultural Understanding." *Signs: Journal of Women in Culture and Society* 5, no. 3 (Spring 1980): 389–417.

Sapir, J. David, and Crocker, J. Christopher, eds. *The Social Use of Metaphor: Essays on the Anthropology of Rhetoric*. Philadelphia: University of Pennsylvania Press, 1977.

Schneider, David M. *American Kinship: A Cultural Account*. 2d ed. Chicago: University of Chicago Press, 1980.

Thompson, Stith. *The Folktale*. New York: Holt, Rinehart and Winston, 1946.

Tilly, Louise A. "Social Sciences and the Study of Women: A Review Article." *Comparative Studies in Society and History* 20 (July 1978):163–73.

Turner, Victor. "Social Dramas and Ritual Metaphors." In his *Dramas, Fields, and Metaphors: Symbolic Action in Human Society*. Symbol, Myth, and Ritual Series. Ithaca, N.Y.: Cornell University Press, 1974.

————. "Social Dramas and Stories about Them." *Critical Inquiry* 7, no. 1 (Autumn 1980):141–68.

Vidich, Arthur J., and Bensman, Joseph. *Small Town in Mass Society: Class, Power, and Religion in a Rural Community*. Princeton, N.J.: Princeton University Press, 1968.

Warner, William Lloyd. *The Living and the Dead: A Study of the Symbolic Life of Americans*. Yankee City Series, vol. 5. New Haven: Yale University Press, 1959.

Wertz, Richard W., and Wertz, Dorothy C. *Lying-in: A History of Childbirth in America*. New York: Free Press, 1977.

Wilson, Margaret Gibbons. *The American Woman in Transition: The Urban Influence, 1870–1920*. Contributions in Women's Studies, no. 6. Westport, Conn.: Greenwood Press, 1979.

INDEX

Altic, Mattie, 36–40 *passim*
Anecdotes: train agent's fear, 26; train porter's fear, 26; mailman's fear, 26–27; Belle Gunness's bust, 33

Babcock, Barbara, 153n19
Ballads, 81, 82, 111, 131, 145–50
Banner, Louise, 65, 66
Barlag, Martin, stories of, 9–10, 38–40, 41, 112
Beauty, changing conceptions of, 61–66
Blake, Louis, stories of, 130
"Bluebeard": folktale plot of, 71; definition of, 151n1; mentioned, 68, 82, 87, 89, 105. *See also* "The Lady Bluebeard"
Bowell, Coroner Bo, 107–108
Bricolage, 13, 143
Bricoleurs, 8, 143
Burns, Eldora Hutson, stories of, 75, 124–25

Chicago, Illinois, 4, 6, 21, 22, 36–43 *passim,* 55, 56–59, 75, 77, 79, 115, 117, 156n5, 160n16
Coffeen, Robert J., stories of, 28, 74, 105, 118
Coffeen, Frank K., stories of, 73–74
Coffeen, Ruth Andrew: stories of, 26; as ballad author, 27–30 *passim,* 81, 108, 131, 146–47

Conspiracy theory, 123–29 *passim,* 135
Corporate system, attitudes toward, 117, 129, 135, 141
Cultural conflict, 26, 40–41, 44, 50–51, 58, 84–85, 90, 139–40
"The culture hero returns" motif, 134
"The culture hero still lives" motif, 118–35 *passim*

Darling, Harry Burr, 21, 118–20, 121
Davis, Carrie Garwood, stories of, 72
Dégh, Linda, and Andrew Vázsonyi, 9
De la Torre, Lillian, 4, 5, 10, 11, 25–26, 59, 128–29, 140–41
Democrats, 19, 122, 129
Deviancy, 11, 35–44, 141–42
Devil, 39
Diesslin, William, 45–49 *passim*
Divorce. *See* Marriage
Dorson, Richard M., 9, 139
Douglas, Mary, 33, 44

Family stories, 11
—Coffeen: anchor rope, 73–74
—Diesslin: Belle Gunness's straying cows, 46–49; her strength after childbirth, 56; her cruelty to their children, 73; her canning human meat, 110–11
—Hutson: Belle Gunness still alive after supposed death, 123–25

171